The Puzzlemaster Presents
Will Shortz's Best Puzzles from NPR®

Volume **2**

Will Shortz
Crossword Editor of *The New York Times*

Introduction by Liane Hansen

Random House
Puzzles & Games

Most of the puzzles that appear in this work were originally broadcast on National
Public Radio's *Weekend Edition Sunday* from 1987 through 2003.

National Public Radio, NPR, Weekend Edition Sunday, and their logos are
registered and unregistered service marks of National Public Radio, Inc.

ISBN: 0-8129-3515-2

Random House Puzzles & Games Web site address:
www.puzzlesatrandom.com

Manufactured in the United States of America

2 4 6 8 9 7 5 3 1

First Edition

INTRODUCTION

When Will Shortz asked me to write an introduction to this second volume of *The Puzzlemaster Presents,* I reacted with one word . . . a nine-letter adjective beginning with D that means highly pleased.*

Several hundred delicious and sometimes diabolical games have been played on the radio since the first volume was published in 1996. Radio is an ephemeral business, however, so there is something very satisfying about capturing these puzzles for a second time in print. It's also a lot of fun to be able to solve them again.

Much is the same since I wrote the introduction to the first volume. The puzzle segment of *Weekend Edition Sunday* is still the high point of many listeners' week. The puzzle is still a constant companion for runners, joggers, and walkers on a Sunday morning, still keeps truckers company on the highway, still keeps folks in bed a little later, still engages whole families at the breakfast table, and still makes people late for church. One minister I met in South Dakota informed me that she had moved the time of her service 10 minutes later to accommodate her puzzling parishioners.

Much has also changed. Close to three million people now listen and play the puzzle every week. When I've been introduced to celebrities—Yo-Yo Ma, Dick Smothers, Hillary Rodham Clinton—they say, "You're the Puzzle Lady," and then proceed to tell me how much they enjoy Will's ingenious word games. Then they say they could NEVER play on the air because it would be too scary. Other celebrities such as Christine Lavin, John Lithgow, and Edie McClurg have welcomed the challenge. I've been told by some folks who've played on the air over the years that they became celebrities in their own right and were written up in their hometown newspapers.

So, for those of you who are novices, and for those of you who've been with us since the beginning, here is another treasure chest of challenges. And remember, when you send in an entry to the program and we call to tell you that you have been chosen to play on the air—fear not. It's only a game.

Liane Hansen

Host, NPR's *Weekend Edition Sunday*

*delighted

ACKNOWLEDGMENTS

Ideas for some of the puzzles in this book come from *Word Ways: The Journal of Recreational Linguistics* (Spring Valley Road, Morristown, NJ 07960) and *The Enigma*, the monthly publication of the National Puzzlers' League (www.puzzlers.org).

I'd like to thank all my friends who tested and polished the puzzles—especially David Rosen, Evie Eysenburg, and Merl Reagle.

Bob Malesky, Wilma Consul, Ned Wharton, and the rest of the talented *Weekend Edition Sunday* crew do a wonderful job of getting the puzzles on the air.

Above all, thanks to Liane Hansen, host extraordinaire of *Weekend Edition Sunday*, and to the listeners, without whom the weekly puzzle would not be possible.

—Will Shortz

1. THE SWITCH IS ON

In each pair of words below, change one letter of each word to *the same new letter of the alphabet* to make two new words that are opposites.

Ex. Fax _____fat_____   Chin _____thin_____

1. Haughty _____   Mice _____
2. Fact _____   Plow _____
3. Puss _____   Foil _____
4. Gender _____   Cough _____
5. Fright _____   Dump _____
6. Bookie _____   Expect _____
7. Air _____   Hinter _____
8. Shorn _____   Call _____
9. Greet _____   Smell _____
10. Breve _____   Scored _____
11. Hose _____   Guess _____
12. Saber _____   Leaded _____

Rating   Good: 8   Excellent: 10   Ace: 12

2. I C CLEARLY NOW

Every answer is a familiar two-word phrase or name with the initials I-C.

Ex. Problem of not knowing who one is _identity crisis_____

1. Main ingredient in a sundae _____
2. Kind of engine _____
3. Hot drink topped with whipped cream _____
4. It used to separate Eastern/Western Europe _____
5. West African country whose capital is Abidjan _____
6. Maize _____
7. Allstate or Aetna _____
8. Its feast is on December 8 _____
9. It might make you feel below everyone else _____

10. Part of the hospital where serious cases go _____

11. Sleuth in "The Pink Panther" movies _____

12. Comedienne who appeared with Sid Caesar on "Your Show of Shows" _____

13. Mathematical invention of Leibniz _____

14. 1934 historical novel set in ancient Rome _____

15. Polaroid _____

16. 3.5" x 5" item that may have speaker's notes _____

17. Business dealings between New York and California, for example _____

18. Group overseeing a president's swearing-in ceremony _____

Rating   Good: 12   Excellent: 15   Ace: 18

3. LOOKING UP

Every answer is a familiar two-word phrase or name in which the initial letters are U-P.

Ex. Person involved in city development ___*urban planner*___

1. News agency ___ International _____

2. Instrument smaller than a baby grand _____

3. Company that helped build the first transcontinental railroad _____

4. Part of Michigan above Lake Michigan _____

5. Like a good golf score _____

6. Rightmost column in an addition problem _____

7. Partner of "cruel," in a phrase _____

8. Publisher of academic books _____

9. Support for telephone wires, cables, etc. _____

10. Insurance that covers everything _____

11. "Airport," "Jaws," "On Golden Pond," and other films made by a particular studio _____

12. What Arrid or Ban stops _____

13. Where nuclear material is processed _____

14. Hawaiian musician _____

15. Planters product with no sodium _____

Rating   Good: 10   Excellent: 12   Ace: 15

4. SCRAMBLED OPPOSITES

Rearrange the letters in the word PANSIES to spell two opposites. For example, you could anagram PANSIES into SIP and SANE—but these aren't opposite in meaning.

5. URBAN SOUNDS

For each of the words below, name a well-known American city that rhymes with it.

   Ex. Flaxen (Mississippi) _____*Jackson*_____
   1. Scenics (Arizona) _____
   2. Prancing (Michigan) _____
   3. Diane (Wyoming) _____
   4. Colder (Colorado) _____
   5. Bruno (Alaska) _____
   6. Clover (Delaware) _____
   7. Noisy (Idaho) _____
   8. Grasper (Wyoming) _____
   9. Palace (Texas) _____
   10. Cargo (North Dakota) _____
   11. Shaken (Georgia) _____
   12. Feeling (West Virginia) _____
   13. Fillings (Montana) _____
   14. Wedding (Pennsylvania or California) _____
   15. Poky (Illinois) _____
   16. Puma (Arizona) _____
   17. Carry (Indiana) _____
   18. Beano (Nevada) _____
   19. Stork (Pennsylvania) _____
   20. Kilo (Hawaii) _____

Rating   Good: 15   Excellent: 18   Ace: 20

6. SHADES OF SEPTEMBER

Every answer here is a two-word phrase containing the consecutive letters S-E-P. Specifically, the first word will end in S-E, and the second word will start with P.

Ex. Sherwin-Williams product that's applied to the outside of a home
_____house paint_____

1. Identification on the front or back of a car _____

2. What seeing a ghost might give you _____

3. What friends may throw for you on your birthday _____

4. Flower part that's a common ingredient in perfume _____

5. Car honking, air horns, and other unwanted sounds _____

6. Waxy implement for writing on glossy surfaces _____

7. Phrase before "hot" and "cold" in a nursery rhyme _____

8. Air-filled snack food that can leave fingers orange _____

9. Item beside a computer _____

10. In a phrase, someone may be led down this _____

11. French scientist after whom a programming language is named
_____

12. Prime-time soap that co-starred Heather Locklear _____

13. Athlete who uses a stick to score a goal _____

14. Telling someone to do something when you want them to do the exact opposite _____

Rating   Good: 8   Excellent: 11   Ace: 14

7. UP TO NO GOOD

Every answer in this puzzle is a word, name, or phrase in which the only consonants are N and G—which may be repeated as often as necessary to answer the clue. Besides N and G, all the letters are vowels. As hints, the lengths of the answers are provided in parentheses.

Ex. Motor (6) _____engine_____

1. Christmas drink (6) _____

2. Nine-sided figure (7) _____

3. Young actress (7) _____

4. Getting older (5) _____

5. Informal term for the head (6) _____

6. Meshing, as gears (8) _____

7. French painter in Tahiti (7) _____

8. Going out in a game of rummy (7) _____

9. Site of the 1998 Winter Olympics in Japan (6) _____

10. Signaling a bad stage act to end (7) _____

11. Real (7) _____

12. Happening (5,2) _____

13. Catching up to, in a race (7,2) _____

14. Reply to a shrew (3,3,3) _____

15. Cry of an auctioneer (5,5,4) _____

Rating   Good: 10   Excellent: 12   Ace: 14

8. STRING QUINTET

The letters E-F-G-H-I can be found consecutively inside the word PRIZEFIGHTER (in mixed order). What familiar word contains the letters L-M-N-O-P consecutively inside it, in any order?

9. DO IT WITH ZEAL

Add the letters Z and L to each word on the left and rearrange the result to spell a new word or name that answers the clue on the right.

Ex. SIT   _LISZT_   Composer Franz

1. HIC   _____   Zero, nada

2. POE   _____   Singer Jennifer

3. BEAR   _____   Tailored jacket that's often blue

4. RAID   _____   Chameleon, e.g.

5. YEAS   _____   Disreputable

6. IBAR   _____   Where Rio de Janeiro is

7. RENO   _____   Broadway lyricist Hart

8. ZONE   _____   Where the water comes out of a hose

9. SUCH   _____   "Peanuts" cartoonist

10. DAVE   _____   Ill-fated ship Exxon ____

11. NEED   _____   Actor Washington

12. TREES _____   Kind of water that effervesces

13. EAGLE _____   Swift animal

14. WASTE _____   Elegant dances

15. RAZED _____   Something that stuns

16. TRIBE _____   Foreign language school

17. ABIES _____   Big

18. PETER _____   It's made with a twist

Rating   Good: 13   Excellent: 16   Ace: 18

10. MOVE TO THE REAR

In this puzzle you are given clues for two five-letter words. Move the first two letters of the first word to the end to get a new word that answers the second clue.

Ex. Like a rainbow ____*arced*____   Hard wood ____*cedar*____

1. Brass or bronze _____   Faithful _____

2. At no time _____   Author Jules _____

3. The "I" of IV _____   Means of commuting _____

4. Viewpoint _____   To find out _____

5. Subject of a lawsuit _____   A famous lawyer _____

6. Sunday dinner _____   Houston ballplayer _____

7. Fancy home _____   Bellini opera _____

8. Pile up _____   Area of India _____

9. A comment in parentheses _____   Thoughts _____

10. Title for Cortés or Pizarro _____   Like Eric the Red _____

11. Kind of dish _____   Worthless stuff _____

12. Mississippi, for example _____   Event on Bikini (hyph.) _____

Rating   Good: 7   Excellent: 9   Ace: 11

11. "8" LINKS

In this puzzle you are given two words. Think of a third word that can precede or follow each of these two to complete compound words or familiar two-word phrases. Hint: Every answer ends in the sound "eight" (in any spelling).

Ex. Board, Roller _____ skate _____
[skateboard, roller-skate]

1. Fair, Department _____
2. Heavy, Paper _____
3. Dinner, Glass _____
4. Shooter, Edge _____
5. Palm, Blind _____
6. Grandmother, Guns _____
7. Exchange, Second _____
8. Clean, Roof _____
9. Show, Fee _____
10. Check, Room _____
11. Train, Air _____
12. Tail, Toll _____

Rating   Good: 7   Excellent: 9   Ace: 12

12. HEAD CASE

Take a familiar nine-letter word and drop its first and last letters to get the names, side by side, of two parts of the human head. What are they?

13. TAKING YOUR CUES

Every answer is a word, name, or phrase beginning with the syllable "Q"—spelled in any way.

Ex. Where Havana is _____ Cuba _____

1. Salad bar vegetable _____
2. Boy with a bow _____
3. Picasso's genre _____

4. Certain cloud _____

5. Certain writing _____

6. Domelike structure on a building _____

7. Skin-related _____

8. Botanical site on the Thames, west of London (2 wds.) _____

9. Actor's aid (2 wds.) _____

10. Actor John, who starred in "The Grifters" _____

11. Company that owns the QE2 _____

12. Tiny office _____

13. Something to hit with a stick (2 wds.) _____

14. Like scores that keep getting added to _____

15. Japanese island southwest of Honshu _____

16. It's at the base of a fingernail _____

17. Kind of doll _____

18. Dollface _____

Rating   Good: 11   Excellent: 14   Ace: 17

14. SHHH!

The answer to the first clue in each pair below starts with the letter J. Change the J to an SH and phonetically you'll get a new word that answers the second clue.

    Ex. Part of a doorway / Fraud

      ___*jamb*___   ___*sham*___

    1. Military vehicle / Animals with wool

      _____   _____

    2. Toast topping / English Romantic poet

      _____   _____

    3. Part of a radio ad / Something a lawyer may have

      _____   _____

    4. Corner square in Monopoly / Layered rock

      _____   _____

5. Collins or Rivers / Displayed

_____   _____

6. Full of ennui / Like things under an umbrella

_____   _____

7. Schmuck / Evade, as responsibility

_____   _____

8. Projecting outward / Closing

_____   _____

9. Use a crowbar on / Ragtime dance

_____   _____

10. Dr. of fiction / Biblical coin

_____   _____

11. Baby kangaroo / Ostentatious

_____   _____

12. Wild dogs that scavenge / Prisoner restraints

_____   _____

Rating   Good: 7   Excellent: 10   Ace: 12

15. S & L

In this puzzle, every answer is a familiar word, name, or phrase in which the only consonants are S and L, repeated as often as necessary. All the other letters are vowels. The lengths of the answers are provided in parentheses.

Ex. Latin dance music (5) ___ *salsa* ___

1. Cowboy's rope (5) _____

2. Tennis star Monica (5) _____

3. ___ Island, immigrants' place (5) _____

4. Fine thread from which knit goods are made (5) _____

5. Dog of 1950s-60s TV (6) _____

6. To attack vigorously or violently (6) _____

7. Person who rents (6) _____

8. Actor Nielsen (6) _____

9. French for "sun" (6) _____

10. Explorer who claimed the Louisiana Territory for France (2,5)
_____

11. Serving no purpose (7) _____

12. Important coal region of Poland (7) _____

13. Ethiopian emperor Haile (8) _____

14. Phrase used to put off making a commitment (3,3) _____

15. By custom (2,5) _____

16. November 2nd, ___ Day (3,5) _____

Rating   Good: 10   Excellent: 13   Ace: 15

16. AUTHOR! AUTHOR!

Take the last name of a famous American writer in seven letters. Change the second letter to a G and you'll name a famous British writer. Who is it?

17. ANALOGIES

In this puzzle, provide the word that will complete each analogy. Every answer involves wordplay of some sort, and each one's logic is different.

Ex. Option : Potion :: Arrest : _____*rarest*_____ [switch first two letters]

1. Mar : Sheep :: Gats : _____

2. Uprise : Downfall :: Undergo : _____

3. Coconut : Dodo :: Gagarin : _____

4. Freight : Octagon :: Canine : _____

5. German : Manger :: Ingrid : _____

6. Sent : Tennessee :: Imps : _____

7. Puddle : Ping-Pong :: Mullet : _____

8. Beat : Attend :: Goon : _____

9. Ohms : Pint :: Star : _____

10. Chocolate : Moose :: Missing : _____

11. Hasten : Greece :: Animal : _____

Rating   Good: 4   Excellent: 7   Ace: 10

18. CONNECTING A TO B

Every answer is a familiar two-word phrase in which the first word ends with the letter A and the second word begins with B.

Ex. Ingredient in suntan lotions *Cocoa butter*

1. Vegetable named for a city in Peru _____

2. Leading dancer in a ballet company _____

3. Piece of furniture that can be converted for sleeping _____

4. Device that answers questions at parties _____

5. Someone who loves "Carmen" and "Aida" _____

6. Black-and-white animal from China given to the Washington Zoo _____

7. The Northern Lights _____

8. Fund of information in a computer _____

9. It might help a defendant get a reduced sentence _____

10. It's used to carry a Nikon or Kodak _____

11. California city that was once the setting of a daytime soap opera _____

12. Home of the N.F.L.'s Buccaneers _____

13. Annual college football game held in Tempe, Arizona _____

14. Georgia ball club that won the World Series in 1995 _____

15. Tiny annoyance for a dog _____

16. Musical group that plays Polish dance tunes _____

17. Competitor of the World Book _____

18. Florida city known for auto racing _____

19. It cools an ocean's shore _____

20. Pants worn to bed _____

Rating   Good: 13   Excellent: 17   Ace: 20

19. ION DISPLAY

Each of the following sentences contains two blanks. Add the letters I-O-N to the end of the word that goes in the first blank to get a new word that goes in the second blank to complete the sentence.

Ex. Following the storm, the ship came into ___*port*___ with a ___*portion*___ of its mast missing.

1. At the riding stable, a mare should not be put in the same _____ as a _____.

2. Sister Mary-Louise from our local _____ was a delegate at last year's political _____.

3. Be sure not to _____ the launch of the first space _____ to Mars.

4. Rep. Quackenbush is sponsoring a _____ to spend several _____ dollars on a highway in his district.

5. Many skin _____ enjoy exploring underwater caves for _____.

6. The polka musicians were all in _____ that what they needed was a new _____ player.

7. The hard-hearted naval officer in charge of the _____ showed little _____ for his fellow crewmen.

8. On many occasions former President Bush still _____ his _____ to broccoli.

9. At the religious breakfast, the ministers were served eggs _____ immediately after the _____.

Rating   Good: 6   Excellent: 8   Ace: 9

20. NICKNAMES

The word HERBAL consists of two consecutive men's nicknames—HERB and AL. Can you think of a familiar *eight*-letter word that consists of two consecutive men's nicknames? Hint: The names begin with R and C, respectively.

21. SPINNING LP'S

In this puzzle, every answer is a word, name, or phrase in which the only consonants are L and P. Hint: The letter Y is not used.

Ex. Part of a suit jacket ___*lapel*___

1. Part of the eye _____

2. 1960s NASA program _____

3. Fill with horror _____

4. What you might do after a bad court decision _____

5. Bad multicar accident _____

6. Rival of Us magazine _____

7. Spanish dish with chicken, seafood, and rice _____

8. Sucker _____

9. Exercise done on a chinning bar (hyph.) _____

10. It's taken to increase one's energy (2 wds.) _____

11. Malt beverage with a light color (2 wds.) _____

12. Sounds made by Alka-Seltzer (2 wds.) _____

13. Head of the Roman Catholic Church from 1963 to 1978 (2 wds.)
    _____

14. Along with mom, it's a symbol of Americanism (2 wds.) _____

15. Place to swim back and forth (2 wds.) _____

16. 15th-century Italian painter with the title "Fra" (2 wds.) _____

Rating   Good: 11   Excellent: 13   Ace: 15

22. WHOSE WHAT?

In this puzzle, each answer is a phrase consisting of the possessive form of a famous person's last name plus the uncapitalized word you get when you drop the name's first and last letters.

Ex. Patrick's victory ___*Ewing's win*___

1. William Randolph's listening devices _____

2. Ringo's road-surfacing material _____

3. Garth's chess piece _____

4. Marlon's South African money _____

5. Fred's way up _____

6. Peter's hammer or saw _____

7. Edgar Lee's flower _____

8. Donald's alcohol _____

9. Danny's ardor _____

10. William's beginner _____

11. Leon's light color _____

12. Juliet's lines of plants in the garden _____

13. Diana's British coins _____

14. Farley's place to raise cattle _____

15. Timothy's singing voice _____

16. Davy's firework _____

17. Lloyd's line of mountains _____

18. Raymond's CB name _____

Rating   Good: 12   Excellent: 15   Ace: 18

23. MOTHER'S DAY

In this Mother's Day puzzle, every answer is a seven-letter word or name that is formed from the letters of MOTHER'S DAY. The initial letter of each answer is provided.

Ex. Means of doing things (M) ___*methods*___

1. Massachusetts college or its town (A) _____

2. To ruin or wipe out (D) _____

3. Listening range (E) _____

4. Small, furry pet (H) _____

5. Leader of an orchestra (M) _____

6. Like peanuts at a carnival (R) _____

7. Russian breed of dog with long, white hair (S) _____

8. Combine chemically with water (H) _____

9. Clothes, slangily (T) _____

10. West African country now called Benin (D) _____

11. Opposite of boastfulness (M) _____

12. In the indefinite future (S) _____

13. Container that keeps liquids hot (T) _____

14. Celebrity status (S) _____

15. Most difficult (H) _____

Rating   Good: 11   Excellent: 13   Ace: 15

24. P.U.

If you put the letters W-O in front of the word MAN, you get the word's opposite, WOMAN. What word becomes its own opposite when you put the letters P-U in front of it?

25. RADIO DIAL

The letters FM can stand for "frequency modulation." They're also the initials of many other familiar two-word phrases. Find the phrases that match the following clues.

Ex. Company that makes the Lincoln and Mercury *Ford Motor*

1. Letters to a celebrity _____
2. Fine steak _____
3. Place to buy and sell used items _____
4. Gold Medal factory _____
5. Bills, but not coins _____
6. Feature of capitalism _____
7. Protective wear for a baseball catcher _____
8. Early term for an airplane _____
9. Pete Seeger and Woody Guthrie genre _____
10. Its defense inspired Francis Scott Key to write "The Star Spangled Banner" _____
11. Mustache with long, droopy ends _____
12. When the Supreme Court convenes in October _____
13. Publicly traded, federally backed security _____
14. What a general practitioner practices _____
15. Person who oversees a building's safety code _____
16. Relaxing rub of the lower extremity _____
17. Cabinet member in other countries who oversees diplomatic relations _____
18. Stage show in which the performers show everything _____

Rating   Good: 12   Excellent: 15   Ace: 18

26. 4 X 4

For each four-letter word below, think of a familiar two-word phrase, both words having four letters, in which the first two letters of the clue word are the first two letters of your first word, and the last two letters of the clue word are the first two letters of your second word.

Ex. BASE ___back seat___ [BAck SEat]

1. GASH _____
2. LOIN _____
3. SLAW _____
4. FALA _____
5. ROBE _____
6. SHAH _____
7. BOSH _____
8. LISP _____
9. LONE _____
10. LAST _____

Rating   Good: 6   Excellent: 8   Ace: 10

27. RH FACTOR

In this puzzle, every answer is a familiar two-word phrase, title, or name with the initials R-H.

Ex. Where a western farmer lives ___ranch house___

1. Something that's deliberately misleading _____
2. Place of convalescence for the elderly _____
3. What most people write with _____
4. One who drives in two lanes, maybe _____
5. Hero in Sherwood Forest _____
6. Child's toy with a saddle and reins _____
7. It might be used to water the lawn _____
8. Jewish High Holy Day _____
9. Title for a prince or princess _____

10. "The _____ Picture Show" _____

11. Measure of water vapor in the air, as expressed in weather forecasts _____

12. What a square peg has trouble fitting in _____

13. When traffic is most congested _____

14. Person who's done something in the fastest time, for example _____

15. School attended by Archie and Jughead _____

16. Rival of Simon and Schuster _____

Rating   Good: 11   Excellent: 13   Ace: 15

28. PROFESSIONAL MIX-UP

Name a profession in 14 letters, in which the first letter is A and an O appears somewhere else in the word. If you're thinking of the right profession, you can drop the O and rearrange the remaining 13 letters to spell the plural of another profession. What is it? Hint: The 13-letter word starts with P.

29. FILM ADAPTATION

Some movies that have won Oscars for Best Picture are listed below … but one word in each title has been anagrammed. You name the movies.

Ex. The Shingle Patient   *The English Patient*

1. The License of the Lambs _____

2. From Here to Entirety _____

3. In the Heat of the Thing _____

4. Cinerama Beauty _____

5. Ascend with Wolves _____

6. Iran Man _____

7. The Nodus of Music _____

8. Inane Hall _____

9. Corky _____

10. Thelma _____

In the following answers, the anagram consists of two or more words that reduce to one word when solved.

11. My Rat _____

12. USA Made _____

13. Not Alpo _____

14. A Dry Iron People _____

15. New Le Car of Arabia _____

16. The Death Frog _____

17. Avert Rehab _____

18. On the Rafter Town _____

Rating   Good: 13   Excellent: 16   Ace: 18

30. TRIPLE RHYME

Answer each clue with a made-up phrase consisting of three consecutive rhyming words.

Ex. Monarch of fancy parties ____wingding king____

1. Award on a wall for winning a game of twenty-one
_____

2. Fancy dress to wear in the central business district
_____

3. Seven days in which to get an advance look at movies
_____

4. Timepiece for Howard Stern, for example _____

5. One who steals recipe volumes _____

6. It weighs letters at the post office _____

7. Cape Canaveral, in the 1960s, when the U.S. was competing with the Soviet Union to put a man on the moon _____

8. Man wooing an ordinary-looking woman _____

9. Expo for computer programs that you can get over the Internet
_____

10. Ballad in a former English colony of China _____

11. Plan by the U.S. basketball team in the Olympics _____

12. An exchange between sites with stolen cars _____

13. Distance from the floor to a bulb providing nocturnal illumination
    _____

14. Something to nosh on in a hiker's bag _____

Rating   Good: 8   Excellent: 11   Ace: 14

31. SOMETHING I OWE

Every answer in this puzzle is a two-syllable word or phrase in which the syllables end in the vowel sounds I and O in that order.

Ex. Printer's goof _____ *typo* _____

1. Farm building _____

2. African animal with a horn _____

3. Spinning toy _____

4. Common dog's name _____

5. Fuel for a funny car _____

6. 1862 Civil War battle site, in Tennessee _____

7. 1960 Alfred Hitchcock film _____

8. Beginner _____

9. Big name in auto insurance _____

10. County in Northern Ireland _____

11. Water power, informally _____

12. Slang term for an arsonist _____

13. World capital in a Woody Allen title _____

14. Nurse's syringe _____

15. A lush _____

16. Mischievous trick; also, in myth, a queen of Carthage, who killed herself when abandoned by Aeneas _____

The following are all hyphenated or two-word answers:

17. Modern exercise system _____

18. Variety of poker _____

19. Its main ingredients are flour, shortening, and sugar _____

20. Cry from the Seven Dwarfs _____

Rating   Good: 12   Excellent: 16   Ace: 19

32. GEOGRAPHICAL PARTS

Name a particular country in eight letters. Remove the name of a body part in left-to-right letters (not necessarily consecutive). The remaining letters will spell another body part in left-to-right letters (not necessarily consecutive). What country is it, and what are the body parts?

33. L.A. DREAMING

Every answer in this puzzle is a familiar two-word phrase, name, or title in which *each word* contains the consecutive letters L-A.

Ex. What you might eat the first course of a meal from ___salad plate___

1. Religious leader of Tibet _____

2. Site of the 1932 and 1980 Winter Olympics, in upstate New York

    _____

3. Star of the movie "Shane" _____

4. Electronic security system for a house or bank _____

5. Astronomical phenomenon that might affect telecommunications on earth

    _____

6. Fundamental principle of quantum mechanics _____

7. Milan's opera house _____

8. Singapore is at its southern tip _____

9. Singer with the 1965 hit "Downtown" _____

10. Where you might learn "amo, amas, amat" _____

11. Christmas decorations, e.g., in front of your house _____

12. Where Britain and Argentina fought a 1980s war _____

13. Athlete who holds a stick with a net _____

14. Manpower used to build the Egyptian pyramids _____

15. It decimated London's population in 1665 _____

16. Where the winner of the booby prize finishes _____

Rating   Good: 9   Excellent: 12   Ace: 15

34. OPPOSITE ENDS

For each of the words given, supply an opposite that ends in the same two letters as the given word. Prefixes like non-, un-, dis-, etc., are not allowed.

Ex. North ___*south*___

1. First _____
2. Near _____
3. Well _____
4. Over _____
5. Major _____
6. Birth _____
7. Leave _____
8. Dawn _____
9. Host _____
10. Tense _____
11. Solid _____
12. Scare _____
13. Unite _____

The following answers end in the same three letters:

14. Hire _____
15. Select _____
16. Give _____
17. Hurry _____
18. Reveal _____
19. Inept _____

The last answer ends in the same four letters:

20. Mother _____

Rating   Good: 13   Excellent: 16   Ace: 19

35. R.N.'S

The letters R.N. stand for "Registered Nurse." But they're also the initial letters of many other phrases. Answer the clues for familiar two-word phrases with the initials R-N.

Ex. What a nasty comment might strike ___raw nerve___

1. Not a pseudonym _____
2. X for 10, or C for 100 _____
3. Its ships fly the Union Jack _____
4. This very instant _____
5. What a G.O.P. presidential hopeful seeks _____
6. Green Party presidential candidate of 2000 _____
7. In the spring it holds pale blue eggs _____
8. 1000, for example, rather than 999 or 1001 _____
9. Book genre that Barbara Cartland was famous for _____
10. Symptom of a cold or flu _____
11. Group of stations that broadcast together _____
12. 1950s and '60s heartthrob who sang "Be-Bop Baby" _____
13. First U.S. president to travel to China _____
14. Drink with Scotch and Drambuie _____
15. What kidnappers send the kidnappee's family _____

Rating   Good: 11   Excellent: 13   Ace: 15

36. DISPLAYING LEADERSHIP

Take the name HARDING, as in Pres. Warren G. Harding. Using just these seven letters, and repeating them as often as necessary, name a famous foreign leader—first and last names, 12 letters altogether. Who is it?

37. A LITTLE T.L.C.

Below are three words starting with the letters T, L, and C. For each set, supply a fourth word that can follow each of these to complete a compound word or a familiar two-word phrase.

Ex. Tootsie, Log, Cake _____roll_____ [Tootsie roll, log-roll, cake roll]

1. Tin, License, Collection _____

2. Taco, Liberty, Cow _____

3. Traffic, Lime, Candle _____

4. Taste, Litmus, Crash _____

5. Trade, Labor, Credit _____

6. Tinder, Letter, Chatter _____

7. Trump, Leisure, Class-action _____

8. Tree, Lap, Counter _____

9. Tea, Lip, Car _____

10. Turtle, Leather, Crew _____

Rating   Good: 6   Excellent: 8   Ace: 10

38. SERVING OF P'S

Each sentence below has two blanks. Think of a word that can go in the first blank whose last letter can be changed to a P to get a new word that goes in the second blank to complete the sentence.

Ex. To cut the ___*grass*___ neatly, you'll have to ___*grasp*___ the mower's handle firmly.

1. To test the ripeness of a melon, place your _____ on its rind and _____ it with your forefinger.

2. The cowboy put on his ten-_____ hat and rode off at a _____.

3. If I ever see you _____ in self-pity, I'm going to _____ you good.

4. It is _____ lunacy to try to make a _____ an indoor pet.

5. An Indian religious teacher, like a _____, is said to know everything—but don't _____ him with questions.

6. When you use a classroom projector, your transparent _____ will naturally _____ the sides of the machine.

7. The crop-spraying pilot will take his pet _____ when he begins to _____ from field to field.

8. [Three words, the last one ending in P:] An experienced deep-sea diver has seen his _____ of _____ bites—so he knows he must always stay _____.

Rating   Good: 4   Excellent: 6   Ace: 8

39. ON YOUR TOES

Every answer here is a word of two or more syllables that is accented on the syllable "toe" (in any spelling).

Ex. Hormone that regulates biorhythms ___melatonin___

1. Month when the World Series is held _____

2. Bad breath _____

3. Yes-man _____

4. ___ Springs, New York _____

5. Neighbor of Ghana _____

6. Japanese general in W.W. II _____

7. Requirement to ride a subway, maybe _____

8. Former chess champion Karpov _____

9. River near the Lincoln Memorial _____

10. Something that's written below a line _____

11. Indian emblem _____

12. Volcano that erupted violently in 1883 _____

13. It's north of North Dakota _____

14. Book of the Apocrypha _____

15. Florida speedway site _____

16. Big, tubular pasta _____

Rating   Good: 9   Excellent: 12   Ace: 15

40. A CAPITAL IDEA

Name a world capital in eight letters. Change its last letter to the next letter of the alphabet, and phonetically you'll get a new word that names something people watch on TV. What is it?

41. SO TH-TH-THERE!

Each sentence below has two blanks. Add -TH to the end of the word that goes in the first blank to get, phonetically, a new word that goes in the second blank to complete the sentence.

Ex. Actress _____Faye_____ Dunaway had _____faith_____ in her director.

1. The lucky Oklahoman used his oil _____ to gain great _____.

2. Drinking too much hot _____ may stain your _____.

3. Rachel tied a _____ on _____ her Christmas presents.

4. The criminals were so sloppy they'd left a _____ of clues for the _____.

5. The _____ members of the barbershop quartet put _____ some beautiful music.

6. In the Christmas play, one of the Wise Men dropped his _____, causing great _____ in the audience.

7. Letting your workout routine go to _____ will have serious consequences to your _____.

8. If that woman _____ her watchdog on you, you'll get bitten in less than a _____ of a second.

9. John has _____ horses on his ranch for many years, giving him great _____ of knowledge in the field.

10. When the female pig got cold in the winter, Farmer Jones would drive the _____ _____.

Rating   Good: 7   Excellent: 9   Ace: 10

42. THE LIVING END

In this puzzle every answer contains the consecutive letters E-N-D. To be precise, the answer is a hyphenated word or two-word phrase in which the first part ends in the letters E-N and the second part starts with D.

Ex. Carpenter's pin   wooden dowel

1. One week _____

2. Invitation to enter a room _____

3. What you do to the hatches _____

4. Rum cocktail served with finely crushed ice _____

5. Variety of apple _____

6. Overtime period in which the first team to score wins _____

7. Whom Abraham Lincoln debated in 1858 _____

8. Frankfurter made from the meat of a fowl _____

9. Jewish star _____

10. Widow of a king _____

11. Prime minister's address in London _____

12. Where a can-opener and eating utensils are kept _____

13. Pulitzer-winning author of "Advise and Consent," 1960
_____

14. Comedienne who came out on her sitcom _____

15. Pumpkins, witches' costumes, orange crepe paper, etc.
_____

16. Brand of ice cream _____

Rating   Good: 9   Excellent: 12   Ace: 15

43. ALLITERATIVE FOURS

Every answer here is a familiar two-word phrase in which both words have four letters and both words start with the same letter of the alphabet.

Ex. 60 inches __five feet__

1. Popular TV drama about the White House, with "The" _____

2. Glass cylinder in a lab _____

3. It has eight sides _____

4. Monday to Friday, for most people _____

5. Amorous relations _____

6. Modern cause of nasty acts by drivers _____

7. Gambler's guiding angel _____

8. A goner _____

9. "___ and prosper" (comment by Mr. Spock on "Star Trek") _____

10. Lather _____

11. What you have in your heart for someone you like _____

12. What an adult must pay for an airplane ticket _____

Rating   Good: 7   Excellent: 10   Ace: 12

44. SWEARING-IN

The word INAUGURATION contains the letters of GNU (three letters), GOAT (four letters), and IGUANA (six letters). What is the longest animal name you can find in INAUGURATION? (No letter can be used in the answer more often than it appears in INAUGURATION.)

45. "U.S." GEOGRAPHY

Every answer in this puzzle is the name of a place in the United States that contains the consecutive letters U-S.

Ex. A U S T I N , Texas

1. _ _ _ _ _ _ U S, Ohio

2. _ _ _ U S _ _, Maine

3. _ _ _ _ _ U S _, New York

4. _ _ U S _ _ _, Texas

5. _ U S _ _ _ _ _ _, Alabama

6. _ _ _ _ U S _ _, Ohio

7. _ U S _ _ _ _, Oklahoma

8. _ _ _ _ _ _ _ U S _ _ _ _ [state]

9. _ U S _ _ _ _ _ _ _ _ [river in New York, Pennsylvania, and Maryland]

10. _ U S _ _ _ _ _ [mountain in South Dakota]

Rating   Good: 5   Excellent: 8   Ace: 10

46. KNEE-HIGH

In this puzzle every answer is a word or name with the accented syllable "knee" (in any spelling).

Ex. Household blinds _venetians_

1. Swiss city famous for peace talks _____

2. One of Columbus's ships _____

3. Conductor Arturo _____

4. "Little" king of early comics _____

5. Lacking vitality _____

6. Japanese stock index _____

7. Actor who starred in "Schindler's List" _____

8. Dictator Mussolini _____

9. Not this one or that one _____

10. Native of the South Seas _____

11. Rival of Honda _____

12. Gas used in outdoor lights _____

13. Emperor accused of setting fire to Rome _____

14. "Girl from ___" (1964 song hit) _____

15. Hero in the Trojan War _____

16. Tattooist's instrument _____

17. Disguised _____

18. Name in "A Christmas Carol" _____

Rating   Good: 11   Excellent: 15   Ace: 18

47. CPR EXAM

You're given three words starting with the letters C, P, and R. Name a fourth word that can follow each of these to complete a compound word or a familiar two-word phrase.

Ex. Check, Play, Rule _**book**_ [checkbook, playbook, rule book]

1. Cold, Permanent, Radio _____

2. Cannon, Puff, Racquet _____

3. Candle, Pilot, Red _____

4. Checker, Peg, Running _____

5. Calling, Post, Registration _____

6. Coffee, Porter, Ranch _____

7. Court, Powder, Reading _____

8. Card, Periodic, Round _____

9. Coast, Point, Rear _____

10. Cap, Pop, Ray _____

Rating   Good: 6   Excellent: 8   Ace: 10

48. ON A FIRST-NAME BASIS

The first syllable of the word BEAGLE sounds like a letter of the alphabet—B. Change this phonetically to the next letter of the alphabet and you get the name SEGAL. Now, think of a common boy's name in two syllables, in which the first syllable sounds like a letter of the alphabet. Change this phonetically to the next letter of the alphabet to get a common girl's name. What names are these?

49. BLANKETY-BLANK

Every answer here is a phrase in the form "___ and ___," where each blank represents a five-letter word. One letter in each word has been changed. What are the phrases?

Ex. Block & whine ___*black & white*___

1. Bribe & gloom _____

2. House & muggy _____

3. Largo & smell _____

4. Flash & blond _____

5. Shout & swept _____

6. Trick & wield _____

7. Broad & waver _____

8. Depth & tapes _____

9. Poker & fight _____

10. Peach & quilt _____

11. Eight & prong _____

12. Rouge & reads _____

13. Twixt & short _____

14. Paint & clock _____

Rating   Good: 8   Excellent: 12   Ace: 14

50. TRIPLE THREAT

In this puzzle you're given clues to some fanciful phrases. In each answer the first syllable is said three times in a row.

Ex. A very active errand-runner _____*go-go gofer*_____

1. One who transports a Hawaiian dress _____

2. Chanteuse at a New York state prison _____

3. Alpine song about a string toy _____

4. Crazy cents-off certificate _____

5. Where stupid, extinct birds lived _____

6. Likely person to do a French line dance _____

7. Huge conflagration of chocolate candies _____

8. New England soup for a Chinese dog _____

9. Very stylish Australian girl _____

10. Flower made with an error and worn on the lapel _____

11. A very enthusiastic critic Ebert _____

12. Idea that's taboo _____

13. One who selects a toy train _____

In the final answer, the first two syllables are repeated three times:

14. Australian animal in a city in Washington _____

Rating   Good: 10   Excellent: 12   Ace: 14

51. A "NEW" PUZZLE

Every answer in this puzzle is a hyphenated word or a familiar two-word phrase that contains the consecutive letters N-E-W, with N-E ending the first part and W starting the next.

Ex. Periodic oscillation in physics ____ *sine wave* ____

1. Street sign with an arrow _____

2. Common property barrier in New England _____

3. Riesling or Mosel, e.g. _____

4. Famous old stock brokerage _____

5. Man who prefers to live and work by himself _____

6. Actress who won an Oscar for "The Three Faces of Eve" (and who married Paul Newman) _____

7. To clean clothes, but not by hand _____

8. Noted African-American congresswoman from California
   _____

9. Female doctor in the old West _____

10. Women use them to captivate men _____

11. What oil helps reduce in a car _____

12. Ones who dig for ore or diamonds (they're "United" in a labor union)
    _____

13. It hangs from pole to pole and carries messages _____

14. Words completing the phrase "over and ..." _____

Rating   Good: 8   Excellent: 11   Ace: 14

52. DOUBLE OCCUPANCY

Think of a familiar two-word phrase that names something every driver needs ... and that contains all five vowels (A, E, I, O, and U) exactly twice. Hint: The first word has 10 letters and the second word has 9.

53. TOUCHDOWN!

Each answer is a two-word phrase with the initials T-D.

Ex. It helps you tear off a piece of adhesive ___tape dispenser___

1. Activity in which you click your heels _____

2. What an auto dealer invites you to take in a new car _____

3. Inability to distinguish pitch in musical sounds _____

4. Reason for a filling _____

5. Thick book with names, addresses, and numbers _____

6. What shook the world in a book by John Reed _____

7. A charitable contribution or state taxes, on your I.R.S. form _____

8. 1976 Martin Scorsese film starring Robert De Niro _____

9. What a TV station tells you it's experiencing when a program suddenly stops _____

10. In China it lasted from the years 618 to 907 _____

11. Leader, slangily _____

12. A doctor uses it when you say "ahhh" _____

13. Günter Grass novel, with "The" _____

14. Small marsupial from Down Under _____

15. Harding administration scandal _____

16. Slang term for Thanksgiving _____

Rating   Good: 9   Excellent: 12   Ace: 15

54. LAND SAKES!

Each sentence below contains a blank. Put the name of a country in the blank to complete the sentence in a punny way.

Ex. The most convenient way to store wines is in ___Iraq___. [a rack]

1. The waitress said, "I don't want to _____, but we close in 15 minutes."

2. The highway accident will be plainly visible if _____ your neck.

3. Just because there's a mistake on the "CBS Evening News" doesn't mean that you can _____ Rather.

4. If you really like my food, have _____.

5. It's been 25 years since we've seen each other, _____ believe it?

6. Oddly, when Harold caught big fish, he would neither measure _____ them.

7. The New Testament begins with Matthew, _____, followed by Luke and John.

8. I asked the movie critic, after he criticized the director's first film, "_____ the second one, too?"

9. Any dark brown deck of cards should be fine, but don't play with it if the _____.

Rating   Good: 4   Excellent: 7   Ace: 9

55. SAY WHAT?

Every answer here is a word or name that begins with the syllable "say" (in any spelling).

Ex. Polio vaccine discoverer ___Sabin___

1. Cavalry sword _____

2. Holy _____

3. Massachusetts town where Nathaniel Hawthorne was born _____

4. To enjoy the taste of _____

5. Game show host Pat _____

6. Paul ___, French artist who painted "The Card Players" _____

7. Longtime "60 Minutes" newsman Morley _____

8. Northern animal with a valuable fur _____

9. Popular watch-maker _____

10. Extreme cruelty _____

11. Big name in electronic games _____

12. One under a captain's command _____

13. Like ocean water _____

14. In myth, a part man/part goat figure _____

15. Island nation in the Indian Ocean _____

16. Passover dinner _____

17. Host of TV's "Cosmos" _____

18. Word after "Homo" _____

Rating   Good: 12   Excellent: 15   Ace: 18

56. CHANGE OF LEADERS

The words BARE, CARE, DARE, FARE, HARE, MARE, PARE, RARE, TARE, and WARE differ from each other only in their first letters. Can you name 14 relatively familiar, uncapitalized, four-letter words that do the same? Plurals are not allowed. The answer includes one relatively modern word, first used in the 1960s.

57. ANA-DECLARATIONS

Anagram the statements to complete the last names of these famous people.

Ex. Jack "I LACK SUN" ___Nicklaus___

1. Rush "I HUG LAMB" _____

2. Rocky "I CAN ROAM" _____

3. Dianne "I NET FINES" _____

4. Rodney "I FLED GARDEN" _____

5. Dwight "I SEE HER NOW" _____

6. Thomas "I GO BUG SHARON" _____

7. Richard "I BLAME RANCH" _____

8. Roman "I SANK P.L.O." _____

9. Leonardo "I DO A CRIP" _____

10. Oscar "I MET SHERMAN" _____

11. Roy "I LET STENCH IN" _____

12. Ernest "I WAG MY HEN" _____

13. George "I USE THE GOWNS" _____

14. Kris "I SENT FOR FORKS" _____

Rating   Good: 9   Excellent: 12   Ace: 14

58. GOING OUT ON A LIMB

Every answer below is a familiar two-word phrase that contains the consecutive letters L-E-G, with the first word ending in L-E and the second word starting with G.

Ex. Automobile lubricant ___*axle grease*___

1. Something you chew and blow _____

2. A kind of bread made with unprocessed ingredients _____

3. Where a war is fought _____

4. Kids climb on it in a playground _____

5. Stoves, washers, and big machines, from an economist's standpoint

_____

6. Bill Clinton or George Bush, scholastically speaking _____

7. Device that shoots tiny metal fasteners _____

8. She played Bea Arthur's mother on "The Golden Girls" _____

9. Garden product brand that helps plants get larger _____

10. Dingy and off-white, like clothes that aren't washed well

_____

11. Chess, Monopoly, or Ping-Pong _____

12. A load on a large truck that has a danger of exploding _____

13. Lag in military production between two countries _____

14. Empty chatter _____

15. What a turkey says _____

Rating   Good: 8   Excellent: 11   Ace: 14

59. LONG JUMP

Each sentence below has three blanks. Think of a word to go in the first blank that has a long-A sound. Change that to a long-E sound to get a new word that goes in the second blank. Then change that to a long-I sound and you'll get another word that goes in the third blank to complete the sentence.

Ex. On a ship, a _____mate_____ who doesn't eat _____meat_____
_____might_____ suffer protein loss.

1. Our boat on the _____ sprang a _____, so we bailed water _____ crazy.

2. The _____ roof was pounded hard by the _____, whose dampness left a _____ sheen afterward in the sun.

3. You might scratch a _____ on your toe if you _____ by a rough stone pyramid along the _____.

4. For breakfast I ordered _____ with blueberries and powdered sugar—but some _____ took my plate. _____!

5. If a bakery's bread is _____, you don't have to worry that anyone will _____ it, no matter how fancy the _____ in which it's made.

6. Inside the Democratic convention, no _____ person would be _____ carrying a _____ for an archconservative.

7. At the hair salon, permanent _____ and hair _____ are some of the things that _____ ask for.

8. The gardener removed the _____ from the toolshed with such amazing _____ that the neighbor who _____ on him missed the whole thing.

9. Sometime _____ we'll add a _____ of gas to the engine, which will make the gas can _____.

Rating   Good: 5   Excellent: 7   Ace: 9

60. NAME SQUARE

The following square of four-letter girls' names reads the same across and down:

```
N E L L
E D I E
L I S A
L E A H
```

Can you arrange four four-letter boys' names in the same way so they read across and down the same? Only familiar names should be used.

61. WHO KNEW?

Every answer here is a word, name, or phrase that ends in the syllable "new" (in any spelling).

Ex. Street ___*avenue*___

1. Something to paddle _____

2. Young actress _____

3. Actor Reeves _____

4. Group of attendants for an important person _____

5. 1960s-'70s vice president ____

6. Chief of staff under the first Pres. George Bush _____

7. First prime minister of Burma _____

8. Business income _____

9. Phrase that means "confidentially" _____

10. Question for a pussycat? _____

11. Welcome in Québec _____

12. Person with sudden wealth or importance _____

13. Hindu deity _____

14. Nickname for William Henry Harrison _____

15. Urging for a magazine subscriber _____

Rating   Good: 9   Excellent: 12   Ace: 15

62. THE "F" WORD

In this puzzle every answer involves a familiar phrase in the form "___ & ___," in which the first word starts with the letter F. The end of the phrase is provided as your clue.

Ex. _____Father_____ & son

1. _____ & foremost

2. _____ & square

3. _____ & fortune

4. _____ & fiction

5. _____ & dandy

6. _____ & stream

7. _____ & loose

8. _____ & chips

9. _____ & brimstone

10. _____ & away

11. _____ & games

12. _____ & blood

13. _____ & center

14. _____ & forget

15. _____ & hounds

16. _____ & drink

17. _____ & starts

18. _____ & aft

19. _____ & a day

20. _____ & far between

Rating   Good: 15   Excellent: 18   Ace: 20

63. COLORFUL LANGUAGE

Each answer here is a compound word or a familiar two-word phrase in which the first part is a color and the second part has been anagrammed as shown. Rearrange the letters in the second part to complete the answer.

Ex. Orange BLOW ____Bowl____

1. Pink LIPS _____

2. Purple EARTH _____

3. Crimson DIET _____

4. Yellow GAPES _____

5. Blue DYNAMO _____

6. Red CADRE _____

7. White SEAL _____

8. Brown ARGUS _____

9. Black SILT _____

10. Silver CENSER _____

11. Gray FLOW _____

12. Rose STAPLE _____

13. Gold CORDER _____

14. Green BESTER _____

Rating   Good: 9   Excellent: 12   Ace: 14

64. CHANGE OF APPAREL

Think of a certain two-word phrase that means "criticizing." Change the first letter of the second word from a D to a G and you'll get a new phrase that names an article of apparel. What phrases are these?

65. SAN FRANCISCO

Below are some words starting with with the letter S. For each one provide an opposite beginning with F.

    Ex. Start ___*finish*___

    1. Slow _____

    2. Stale _____

    3. Slavery _____

    4. Smile _____

    5. Skinny _____

    6. Succeed _____

    7. Spring _____

    8. Smart _____

    9. Strong _____

    10. Successor _____

    11. Sterile _____

    12. Stiff _____

    13. Senior _____

    14. Sorority _____

    15. Seldom _____

Rating   Good: 9   Excellent: 12   Ace: 15

66. R. & D.

Every answer in this puzzle is a word in which the only consonants used are R and D, repeated as often as necessary, along with any number of vowels. Lengths of the answers are provided in parentheses.

    Ex. Passion or fervency (5) ___*ardor*___

    1. Library user (6) _____

    2. Blade at the back of a boat (6) _____

3. Polite term for your backside (8) _____

4. Poisonous snake (5) _____

5. Stock up on more goods (7) _____

6. Oakland football player (6) _____

7. German Renaissance artist famous for woodcuts and engravings (5)
_____

8. Air traffic control system (5) _____

9. Sent a message by wireless (7) _____

10. Scoffed or jeered at (7) _____

11. Desperate or all-out, as an attempt (2-2-3) _____

12. Reason for a siren, as in a war (3,4) _____

13. Antlered animal with a ruddy coat (3,4) _____

14. Silence in broadcasting (4,3) _____

15. Place to enter a house when you don't want to be seen (4,4)
_____

This last answer includes the letter Y used as a vowel:

16. First line in a personal journal (4,5) _____

Rating   Good: 10   Excellent: 13   Ace: 15

67. LOOSE ENDS

In this puzzle you are given clues for two words. The answer to the first clue has eight letters. Remove the first and last letters and you'll get a new, six-letter word that answers the second clue.

Ex. Make a mess when hitting the floor / River in Nebraska

_____splatter_____   _____Platte_____

1. Complimenting / Dried grape

_____   _____

2. Kind of conclusion / Beaver State

_____   _____

3. Earthenware / Chair for a grandmother

   _____   _____

4. Like a steak that's black / Actress Gwen of "Damn Yankees"

   _____   _____

5. Wearing Hindu headwear / Cosmopolitan

   _____   _____

6. Without anything to eat / A great many

   _____   _____

7. Least hilly / Starbucks orders

   _____   _____

8. Forest plant (2 wds.) / Illegal cigarette

   _____   _____

9. Scrap / Dealers in cloth scraps

   _____   _____

10. To cross / People who talk insanely

   _____   _____

11. Dangerous rush / Pressed down, as tobacco in a pipe

   _____   _____

12. Tough problem / To amuse

   _____   _____

Rating   Good: 6   Excellent: 9   Ace: 12

68. THE WRITE STUFF

Take the word AUTHOR, add one letter, and rearrange the result to name a famous author. Who is it?

69. QU- QUIZ

Each of the sentences below has two blanks. The word that goes in the first blank begins with the letters QU- pronounced "kw-." Drop the W sound leaving just the "k-" sound at the start, and phonetically you'll get the word that goes in the second blank to complete the sentence.

Ex. The sudden California ____quake____ shook the birthday ____cake____ right off the table.

1. A porcupine _____ won't _____ you, but it sure will hurt.

2. To propagate the royal line, every _____ is _____ to have an heir.

3. Because of the high winds in March, that is _____ a good time to fly a _____.

4. When father caught junior goofing off, he gave him a _____ _____ in the pants.

5. A tricky legal case regarding stolen _____ watches had several _____ tied up.

6. Mother said—and I _____—"Don't forget your winter _____!"

7. I have no _____ about the prisoner holding the crying baby if he successfully _____ the baby down.

8. Teasing Mr. Spock about his purely logical approach to all matters was a popular _____ of Captain _____.

9. We'd never seen anyone _____ like that _____ who was afraid of bats.

10. Several wrong stitches by the _____ threw the whole comforter out of _____.

Rating   Good: 6   Excellent: 8   Ace: 10

70. FOR DEAR OLD DAD

Each sentence has two blanks. Add the letters P-A in front of the word that goes in the first blank to get a new word that goes in the second blank to complete the sentence.

Ex. Sweet-talking the prison officials had no ____role____ in the inmate getting __parole__.

1. The Queen personally chose the _____ window curtains for the _____.

2. You shouldn't play _____ on the Irish on St. _____ Day.

3. After he _____ himself while shaving, the worrier _____ and called a doctor.

4. To get a car _____, a 17-year-old driver may need _____ consent

5. At the Spanish restaurant, _____ Fitzgerald ordered _____.

6. Meanwhile, _____ Turner admired the _____ on her furniture.

7. If you can invent a _____ that can be put up in 30 seconds, you should apply for a _____.

8. We _____ for sea bass just outside the area that the Coast Guard _____.

9. Surrounded by dozens of notables from the art world, the cemetery officials will _____ the celebrated _____ at 4 p.m.

10. It's not nice to _____ [2 wds.] someone who's such a _____ of virtue.

Rating   Good: 6   Excellent: 8   Ace: 10

71. EXPERIENCING THE DT'S

In this puzzle every answer is a familiar word or phrase in which the only consonants are D and T—repeated as often as necessary. The letter Y is not used. Lengths of the answers are provided in parentheses.

Ex. Have original thoughts (6) ____ideate____

1. Lost weight (6) _____

2. Numbskull, dummy, or fool (5) _____

3. Practice piece, in music (5) _____

4. Surpassed (6) _____

5. Obsolete (5) _____

6. Checked for accuracy, as financial books (7) _____

7. Expression meaning "same here!" (5) _____

8. Expressed mild disapproval of (3-6) _____

9. Up until this point (2,4) _____

10. Simple children's puzzle (3-2-3) _____

11. Possible tennis score after deuce (2-3) _____

12. Supplemented (5,2) _____

13. Became extinct (4,3) _____

14. It's stamped inside a library book (3,4) _____

15. Cry of achievement (1,3,2) _____

Rating   Good: 9   Excellent: 12   Ace: 15

72. DIALING 6-8-7

What familiar nine-letter word, if dialed on a telephone, would be represented as 6-8-7-6-8-7-6-8-7?

73. PLAYING LP'S

Every answer here is a familiar two-word phrase with the initials L-P.

    Ex. Trap for catching shellfish ___*lobster pot*___

    1. What every car on the highway needs _____

    2. A bullfrog sits on it _____

    3. Upstate New York town famous for skiing and winter sports

    _____

    4. Teacher of contracts or torts _____

5. Tories' opponents in England _____

6. Nadir _____

7. Safety item on a boat _____

8. What a teacher prepares for each class _____

9. American coin since 1909 _____

10. It's recited in church _____

11. Blast-off site for a rocket _____

12. Correction fluid _____

13. Book by Antoine de St.-Exupéry, with "The" _____

14. Aphrodisiac drink _____

15. Computer product made by Hewlett-Packard _____

16. What a woman experiences during childbirth _____

17. Tiny ornament worn on a jacket _____

18. Furthest from first, in the standings _____

Rating   Good: 11   Excellent: 15   Ace: 18

74. NOTHING LOST

Some sentences are given below, each with two blanks. The word that goes in the first blank begins with O. Remove the O and you'll get the word that goes in the second blank to complete the sentence.

Ex. In the Mideast, a hardy ____olive____ tree can ____live____ for more than 50 years.

1. The sunset appeared in brilliant red, yellow, and _____ over the mountain _____.

2. In my _____, your car should have rack and _____ steering.

3. Scientists are concerned about the disappearance of _____ in a _____ over Antarctica.

4. From a stand near the finish line, an official presented the results _____ for the road _____.

5. In flowers, the location of the _____ can _____ from plant to plant.

6. The actress's tough-guy companion at the _____ had two _____ across his forehead.

7. Our flight was delayed _____ to a problem with one of the _____ engines.

8. In the 1960s, _____ [2 wds.] was an important _____ of a modern museum's holdings.

9. For the Green Berets, a single _____ from their supply list can mean failure for an entire _____.

10. The palm trees are dying and the water is polluted, so the Bedouin is buying the _____ _____ [2 wds.].

Rating   Good: 6   Excellent: 8   Ace: 10

75. RHYME AND REASON

Answer each clue with a word that rhymes with the last word in the clue.

Ex. Foot with a claw _____*paw*_____

1. Wheels for a tyke _____

2. What a bee does _____

3. What mediators produce _____

4. Smelled like a skunk _____

5. Something afloat _____

6. Something used to warn _____

7. Hotel famous for its glitz _____

8. Giving off lots of light _____

9. Edge _____

10. Bread maker _____

11. Walk on, for example _____

12. It goes tick-tock _____

13. Falsify _____

14. Counting them helps you get to sleep _____

15. Tiniest amount spent _____

16. Abominate _____

17. Explorers' goals _____

18. Traveling actors' group _____

19. The sky's hue _____

20. Where water comes out _____

21. Spot _____

22. More than twice _____

23. Stack of wood for a fire _____

24. Bird type _____

25. Fair _____

26. Sound of a bell _____

Rating   Good: 18   Excellent: 23   Ace: 26

76. C-T PLANNING

Think of two words starting with C and ending with T—each containing seven or fewer letters—that are exact opposites in meaning.

77. FOR MOTHER

Clues for two words are given below. Put the letters M-A in front of the answer to the first clue to get the answer to the second clue.

Ex. Monarch / Constructing ____*making*____ [king]

1. Opposite of "that" / Singer Johnny _____

2. Backyard building / Like some potatoes _____

3. Breakfast cereal for kids / Mold from which something is made
_____

4. Bugs in the hair / Ill will _____

5. Person from Glasgow / Team emblem _____

6. Not limber / Big dog _____

7. Kind of boom / Kind of temple _____

8. Hang around / Shirk duties _____

9. Away from the coast / What Massachusetts is to Martha's Vineyard _____

10. In better order / A shark, for example _____

Rating   Good: 6   Excellent: 8   Ace: 10

78. STARTER SWITCH

In this puzzle you are given the first word of a common two-word phrase in which the first two letters of the second word are the same as the first two letters of the first word, only reversed. Identify the second word to complete the phrase. Lengths of the answers are provided in parentheses.

Ex. New (7) __*England*__

1. Absentee (6) _____

2. Carbolic (4) _____

3. Arms (4) _____

4. Mirror (5) _____

5. Usual (8) _____

6. Escort (7) _____

7. Foreign (6) _____

8. Car (8) _____

9. Ninth (6) _____

10. Opium (5) _____

11. Walk (4) _____

12. National (6) _____

13. Mission (10) _____

14. Rap (6) _____

15. Unlisted (6) _____

Rating   Good: 9   Excellent: 12   Ace: 15

79. AUTO ANALYSIS

Change one letter in each word or phrase below to name a part of a car.

Ex. Hold _____*hood*_____

1. Able _____

2. Loco _____

3. Ratio _____

4. Medal _____

5. Wiser _____

6. Brave _____

7. Chose _____

8. Pistol _____

9. Basket _____

10. Render _____

11. Crutch _____

12. Sunroom _____

13. Frights _____

14. Washboard _____

15. Toll bar _____

16. Back beat _____

17. First year _____

18. Spare time _____

Rating　　Good: 12　　Excellent: 16　　Ace: 18

80. F AND E

What two words starting with F and ending with E go together with "and" in the middle to complete a common phrase in the form "___ and ___"?

81. KEEPING YOU ON YOUR TOES

Every answer here is a familiar word or phrase that begins with the syllable "toe" (in any spelling).

Ex. High-protein food ___tofu___

1. Old Roman robe _____

2. Neighbor of Ghana _____

3. Japanese general in World War II _____

4. Answer #3's capital _____

5. Theater award _____

6. Indian post _____

7. Completely wreck _____

8. Fancy garden work _____

9. Oscar-winning actress for "My Cousin Vinny" _____

10. November birthstone _____

11. Group with the 1961 #1 hit "The Lion Sleeps Tonight," with "The"
_____

12. Book of the Apocrypha _____

13. Holy parchment _____

14. Brand of smoker's tooth polish _____

15. Drinker _____

16. Kind of poisoning _____

Rating   Good: 10   Excellent: 13   Ace: 15

82. WHAT'S IN A NAME?

For each description below, name an appropriate celebrity whose name can be found among the letters in the description. Lengths of the answers are provided in parentheses.

Ex. AUTHOR (4) ___ROTH___

1. CONSUMER ADVOCATE (5) _____

2. WRITER/FEMINIST (7) _____

3. MAP CREATOR (8) _____

4. COURT JUSTICE (6) _____

5. TENNIS CHAMPION (4) _____

6. FASHION DESIGNER (4) _____

7. SPORTSCASTER (6) _____

8. DANCE ARTIST (7) _____

9. LOVELORN ADVISOR (7) _____

10. SOPRANO (4) _____

11. GENERAL (3) _____

12. NOVELIST (5) _____

Rating   Good: 5   Excellent: 8   Ace: 11

83. IN FRONT

For each pair of clues, put IN in front of the word that answers the first clue to get a new word that answers the second clue.

   Ex. Unit of paper / To ask

    _____*quire*_____   _____*inquire*_____

1. Cost for college students / Feeling you have

   _____   _____

2. Red flower / Embodiment

   _____   _____

3. Steeple / Fill with hope

   _____   _____

4. What some people keep at their bedside at night / Hires as a long-term worker

   _____   _____

5. Edge / Violate, as legal rights

   _____   _____

The following answers work phonetically rather than by spelling:

6. Smell, for example / What you might smell in a pagoda

   _____   _____

7. Winter coat / Derive from logic

   _____   _____

8. Food made from beans / Ran up, as expenses

   _____   _____

9. Joke / To consume

   _____   _____

10. Wonderful / One who isn't properly thankful

    _____   _____

11. Said "alas!" / Part hidden from view

    _____   _____

12. Like every answer in a crossword puzzle / To have as a part

    _____   _____

Rating   Good: 6   Excellent: 9   Ace: 12

84. ROMAN NUMERALS

Seven letters of the alphabet are also Roman numerals—I, V, X, L, C, D, and M. What is the shortest familiar English word that uses six of these seven letters?

85. PACKING ON THE POUNDS

Every answer in this puzzle is a familiar two-word phrase that starts with L and ends with B.

   Ex. Crustacean that spends most of its time out of the water
   _____ *land crab* _____

   1. What Mary had, in a nursery rhyme _____

   2. Certain punch of a boxer _____

   3. Group that meets regularly for a midday meal _____

4. Part of a lamp _____

5. Angry group that seeks a Wild West sort of justice
_____

6. Be, seem, or look, grammatically _____

7. Red Square attraction _____

8. Place in school where you might practice Spanish
_____

9. Something a seafood eater might put on _____

10. Baby feline in a zoo _____

11. Vehicle for hire _____

12. Dangerous thing to open in the mail _____

The following answers are three-word phrases, still starting with L and ending with B:

13. Star of "The Virginian" on '60s TV _____

14. What you risk when you do something dangerous
_____

Rating   Good: 8   Excellent: 11   Ace: 14

86. TWO TIMES THREE

In this puzzle every answer consists of two three-letter words—starting with the same letter—that go together to make a compound word or a familiar two-word phrase.

Ex. Vegetable holder ___*pea pod*___

1. Teeter-totter _____

2. Walk ver-r-r-ry quietly _____

3. Sty _____

4. It may bite you at night _____

5. Last part of a Casey Kasem countdown _____

6. Foreign correspondent? _____

7. Baseball team assistant _____

8. Conceal oneself, biding one's time _____

9. 1979 Mel Gibson film _____

10. London tourist site _____

11. "Later" _____

12. Cocktail made with Scotch whiskey _____

13. Baked dish with meat and vegetables _____

14. Not seriously _____

15. Last scene in many a western _____

Rating   Good: 9   Excellent: 12   Ace: 15

87. OVERLAPS

In the five-letter word PEARL, the first four letters spell a word (PEAR), and the last four letters spell a word (EARL). Each sentence below has three blanks. The word that goes in the first blank consists of the first four letters of a five-letter word, and the word that goes in the second blank is its last four letters. The final blank is for the five-letter word itself.

Ex. While eating a ____*pear*____, the ____*Earl*____ of Sandwich recalled that he had forgotten to buy a ____*pearl*____ necklace for his wife.

1. The _____ and beautiful princess lived in a high, _____ castle room, according to the _____ tale.

2. The nays from the West outnumbered the _____ from the _____, so the legislative bill on baker's _____ was defeated.

3. Looking _____ is hard for a country _____ to do when he's caring for an injured _____ from the henhouse.

4. The actor playing King _____ could _____ more money if he would only _____ his lines.

5. _____ of Greenwich Village is composed of pretentious, _____ types, which is why I don't like to _____ there.

6. Ladies' _____ made of Himalayan goat fiber might produce a _____ on sensitive skin, so it would be _____ to put one on.

7. A big, _____ guy is a good _____ to have in a fight, because he'll help you _____ more victories.

8. The annual Memorial Day parade auto race will _____ up at _____ on a _____, rain-soaked afternoon.

9. You should put the electric outlet _____ with the air _____, in the _____ you get the decorating job.

10. Cleaning up after an artist is quite a _____, because it _____ easy to get _____ off your clothes.

Rating   Good: 6   Excellent: 8   Ace: 10

88. BEAR SESSION

Consider the phrases "___ bear" and "___ session." Think of a word that can go in the first blank; then change its first letter to the next letter of the alphabet in order to get what goes in the second blank. What is it?

89. ALL ABOUT ME

Every answer below is a familiar two-word phrase with the initials M-E.

Ex. Slender tropical fish _____ *moray eel* _____

1. World's tallest peak _____

2. Where Israel and Lebanon are located _____

3. TV's talking horse _____

4. Person who performs autopsies _____

5. Person who runs a magazine _____

6. Expert on motors _____

7. Canadian baseball player _____

8. Geological period when the dinosaurs reigned _____

9. Something orangeish to mail documents in _____

10. What follows the preliminary contests, as in boxing _____

11. Conflicted feelings _____

12. 1978 Brad Davis film that was a Best Picture nominee _____

13. Our language as it's been spoken since about 1473 _____

14. Exclamation of disbelief _____

15. Something that reading or puzzle-solving provides
    _____

Rating   Good: 9   Excellent: 12   Ace: 15

90. DOUBLE F'S

Unscramble the following words, each of which contains two consecutive F's somewhere inside it.

    Ex. ORE + FF ___OFFER___

    1. SIN + FF _____

    2. AGE + FF _____

    3. ROAD + FF _____

    4. ABLE + FF _____

    5. RITA + FF _____

    6. TUBE + FF _____

    7. TORE + FF _____

    8. LURE + FF _____

    9. ARIA + FF _____

    10. INSET + FF _____

    11. LEMUR + FF _____

    12. POINT + FF _____

    13. CLUES + FF _____

    14. HIRES + FF _____

    15. LOUSE + FF _____

    16. TULANE + FF _____

    17. ARGUES + FF _____

    18. ORATED + FF _____

Rating   Good: 9   Excellent: 14   Ace: 17

91. UPS AND DOWNS

The answer to the first clue in each pair below is a compound word or a common two-word phrase that ends in UP. Change the UP to DOWN and you'll get a new compound word or a common two-word phrase that answers the second clue.

Ex. Playboy feature / To find specifically

_____*pin-up*_____   _____*pin down*_____

1. To improve slightly / Football score

_____   _____

2. Event on a cattle range / Be conservative in estimating

_____   _____

3. Appear, as at an event / Final battle

_____   _____

4. Start to laugh hard / Police action against criminals

_____   _____

5. Robbery / To have, as a job

_____   _____

6. Kind of comedian / To quit, as during a confrontation

_____   _____

7. Thorough change in management / Extortion, as by blackmail

_____   _____

8. Put on fancy clothes / To sharply criticize

_____   _____

9. Divorce / Reason to call for a tow truck

_____   _____

10. Certain exercise / Kind of strike

_____   _____

11. Prankster / Fell, as a tree

_____   _____

12. Order to a noisy person / Cessation of business

_____   _____

Rating   Good: 8   Excellent: 10   Ace: 12

92. FIRST FIVE

The nine-letter word SUBDEACON contains the first five letters of the alphabet (A to E) consecutively inside it, although not in alphabetical order. Similarly, the eight-letter word FEEDBACK contains the first five letters of the alphabet consecutively inside it. What common seven-letter word has this same property?

93. TWO G'S

Every answer in this puzzle is a familiar two-word phrase that starts and ends with G.

Ex. Common greeting _____*good morning*_____

1. Animal that's the subject of experiments _____

2. Zero, in slang _____

3. Result of greenhouse gases _____

4. Possible result of an oil shortage _____

5. It flies over public buildings in Athens _____

6. Old-fashioned way of making bottles _____

7. Service that stores often provide around Christmas

_____

8. Miscellany _____

9. Where a road meets a railroad track _____

10. Command to a little dogie _____

11. Edgar Allan Poe story, with "The" _____

12. Something a stripper wears _____

13. It helps a blind person get around _____

14. Sign on a business that's closed for vacation _____

Rating   Good: 8   Excellent: 11   Ace: 14

94. TRADING PLACES

The answer to the first clue in each pair is a word with the vowels O and A (in that order) somewhere inside. Switch the O and A to A and O and you'll get a new word that answers the second clue.

Ex. The "Rubaiyat" poet / Another name for Cupid

__Omar__   __Amor__

1. A score in soccer / Lockup in England

    _____ _____

2. Spanish greeting / Angel's accessory

    _____ _____

3. Musical instrument / Gas used in fluorescent tubes

    _____ _____

4. Word before "nova" / Certain opera singer

    _____ _____

5. First name in late-night talk / Body of principles

    _____ _____

6. South Seas kingdom / Sensuous dance

    _____ _____

7. Composition of many a South Seas island / Song

    _____ _____

8. Dazzling pictures (2 wds.) / To the left, to a sailor

    _____ _____

9. Mel Gibson, to Danny Glover, in "Lethal Weapon" / Kind of oil

    _____ _____

10. Certain numerical rating / Start of a play (2 wds.)

    _____ _____

Rating   Good: 5   Excellent: 8   Ace: 10

95. IT'S COLD!

Every answer here is a word or name starting with the syllable "brrr!" (in any spelling).

    Ex. Pack animal   *burro*

1. French wine _____
2. Germany's capital _____
3. Low comedy _____
4. Sack material _____
5. Comedienne Carol _____
6. Alabama city _____
7. Vermont city _____
8. Kind of shorts _____
9. Grow rapidly _____
10. Myanmar's former name _____
11. Upper Volta's modern name _____
12. Someone who doesn't belong in your house _____
13. Nuts _____
14. Item between two buns _____
15. British general in the American Revolution _____
16. Inflammation near a joint _____
17. 1960s hit by the Four Tops _____
18. City where "The Tonight Show" is taped _____

Rating   Good: 12   Excellent: 15   Ace: 17

96. WORD'S WORTH

Assign every letter of the alphabet its numerical value: A = 1, B = 2, C = 3, etc., up to Z = 26. The product of the letter values of what common English word is exactly 3,000,000?

97. ANIMAL PENS

For each pair of words below, name an animal that can follow the first word and precede the second one to complete a compound word or a familiar two-word phrase. Note: None of the new words or phrases formed can themselves be animals.

Ex. Cash ___Cow___ Slip

1. Dark _____ Laugh
2. Grease _____ Business
3. Copy _____ Nap
4. Hot _____ Paddle
5. Paper _____ Lily
6. Road _____ Wild
7. Pack _____ Race
8. White _____ Ears
9. Silver _____ Trot
10. Literary _____ Hearted
11. Lone _____ Whistle
12. Mickey _____ Pad
13. Black _____ Skin
14. Bug _____ Left

Rating   Good: 8   Excellent: 11   Ace: 14

98. A PUZZLE? OY!

Each sentence below contains two blanks. The word that goes in the first blank has a long-A sound (as in "bake") somewhere in it. Change that long-A sound to an OI sound (as in "boy") to get a new word that goes in the second blank to complete the sentence.

Ex. No plain ___Jane___ was allowed to ___join___ the top sorority.

1. The teenager downtown said, "See you _____!" … but continued to _____ on the street corner.

2. In the debater's _____ to make a clever reply, he is _____ by his own petard.

3. The apprentice house _____ needed a helpful _____ on how to hold a brush.

4. The blind chef read a recipe in _____ on how to _____ a chicken.

5. The riot police _____ the demonstrators, which immediately made their eyes _____.

6. At the Victorian-style restaurant, there was a _____ change of the _____ underneath each place setting.

7. In the Miss America pageant, self-composure is very important, so it _____ to have _____.

8. The psychoanalyst's nerves were _____ from studying too much _____.

9. The chemistry building at _____ University is installing a new furnace in its _____ room.

10. A film thriller that ends with a _____ scene would not be my first _____ tonight.

Rating   Good: 5   Excellent: 8   Ace: 10

99. M & M'S

Each answer here is a familiar two-word phrase with two consecutive M's inside it—one ending the first word and the other starting the second.

Ex. Cause of a computer breakdown _system malfunction_

1. Head of a marching band _____

2. Dairy drink that's low in fat _____

3. Athletic contest held in a pool _____

4. 1999 "Star Wars" episode, with "The" _____

5. 1960s civil rights protest, involving walking from one city to another _____

6. Leader of the Doors _____

7. Old movie cowboy _____

8. "Cheers" bartender _____

9. In the title of a best-selling book, "Men Are …" what?
_____

10. Branch of physics dealing with atoms and molecules
_____

11. Chemical compound with the symbol Na_2O _____

12. Tractor and thresher, for example _____

13. Goat for Navy, or Tiger for Princeton _____

14. Popular brand of shoes _____

15. President before Theodore Roosevelt _____

Rating Good: 8   Excellent: 12   Ace: 15

100. EVEN OUT

Think of a particular seven-letter adjective starting with the letter B. Remove the second, fourth, and sixth letters to get a four-letter noun that the adjective would describe. What is it?

101. "V" FOR VICTORY

Rearrange the letters in each word below to make a new word starting with the letter V.

Ex. SAVE __VASE__

1. EVER _____

2. IVAN _____

3. RIVAL _____

4. DIVAN _____

5. CAVEAT _____

6. LOVELY _____

7. IRVING _____

8. DEVOTE _____

9. COVERT _____

10. LATVIAN _____

11. OBSERVE _____

12. GUSTAVE _____

13. DOVETAIL _____

14. RELATIVES _____

15. PREDICTIVENESS (hyph.) _____

Rating   Good: 9   Excellent: 12   Ace: 14

102. LEADING SAINTS

Every answer in this puzzle is a familiar two-word phrase with the initials S-T.

Ex. Chit-chat ____ *small talk* ____

1. Golf course hazard _____

2. Old TV show starring William Shatner _____

3. Man's apparel for a beach or pool _____

4. Extra amount added to a purchase price _____

5. Item in a car trunk _____

6. Marine animal with a shell _____

7. Chang and Eng, famously _____

8. Person who is easily convinced or imposed upon _____

9. Brass instrument with a moving part _____

10. Love of candy _____

11. Preseason baseball activity _____

12. Group of eleven players, including a goalie _____

13. Person whom students traditionally play tricks on _____

14. Uncooked meat dish _____

15. The tulip poplar to Tennessee, for example _____

Rating   Good: 8   Excellent: 12   Ace: 15

103. T-SER

There are many common two-word phrases in which both words begin with T, like "tulip tree" and "tube top." In this puzzle, the second word of a common "T— T—" phrase is given. You provide the first. Hint: None of the answers begins with "th-."

    Ex. Tack ____*tie*____ [tie tack]

    1. Trove _____

    2. Tantrum _____

    3. Tennis _____

    4. Typist _____

    5. Twister _____

    6. Twos _____

    7. Track _____

    8. Tag _____

    9. Tube _____

    10. Truck _____

    11. Ten _____

    12. Trap _____

    13. Travel _____

    14. Trot _____

Rating   Good: 8   Excellent: 11   Ace: 14

104. THAT'S ENTERTAINMENT

Think of a well-known modern actor who has three letters in his first name and seven letters in his last. His first and last names rhyme, respectively, with the first and last names of a famous entertainer of the past. The entertainer of the past has five letters in his first name and six letters in his last. What two celebrities are these?

105. BOSTON TALK

In and around Boston, many people pronounce the unaccented "a" at the end of a word as an "er." For example, the word "Cuba" might come out as "cuber." Each of the sentences below has two blanks. The word that goes in the first blank ends in an unaccented "a." Change it to an "er" sound and you'll get a new word that goes in the second blank to complete the sentence.

Ex. After uploading his personal _____data_____ to the online matchmaker program, the previously lonely bachelor became quite an avid _____dater_____.

1. A drugstore employee in _____, Florida, was caught trying to _____ with sealed bottles.

2. The zoo in _____, Peru, just acquired a _____ from Madagascar.

3. Did the _____ Indians of ancient Peru have a primitive _____ for printing documents?

4. In Exodus, the Israelites received _____ from heaven in a very surprising _____.

5. To followers of professional tennis, _____ Seles has a funny _____: "Little Miss Grunt."

6. Since mama wanted some popcorn to snack on while watching home movies, _____ bought her a _____.

7. While munching on a _____ fish sandwich, the piano _____ fixed my Steinway.

8. Dancers in a _____ line weaved around the room like a _____ eel.

9. John bought his girlfriend a huge black-and-white _____ in a base attempt to _____ to her love for stuffed animals.

10. The jokes told by the ophthalmologist, who specialized in the _____, are _____ than those told by the retina specialist.

Rating   Good: 5   Excellent: 8   Ace: 10

106. TWO TO THREE

For each two-syllable word below, provide a common, uncapitalized three-syllable word that both rhymes with it and starts with the letter indicated. (In order to rhyme, your word will have to be accented on the second syllable.)

    Ex. Patrick (T) ___theatric___

    1. Coma (D) _____

    2. Pony (B) _____

    3. Dormant (I) _____

    4. Fossil (A) _____

    5. Cotton (F) _____

    6. Scruple (Q) _____

    7. Vermin (D) _____

    8. Rival (S) _____

    9. Virus (P) _____

   10. Thistle (E) _____

   11. Stanza (B) _____

   12. Region (C) _____

   13. Pennant (L) _____

   14. Tepid (I) _____

   15. Buoyance (C) _____

   16. Bludgeon (C) _____

Rating   Good: 9   Excellent: 13   Ace: 16

107. ALL LIES

Every answer in this puzzle starts with the syllable "lie," in one spelling or another. As a special twist, every clue contains a factual inaccuracy!

    Ex. Animal that's Princeton's mascot ___Lion___
        [The Lion is Columbia's mascot; Princeton's mascot is the Tiger]

    1. Procter & Gamble disinfectant _____

2. Spoken defamation _____

3. The plus side of a balance sheet _____

4. Flower named in Whitman's elegy to Daniel Webster _____

5. Kind of bean with red pods _____

6. Slang term for a French sailor _____

7. Noted literary critic Jeffrey _____

8. Institution that uses the Adm. Dewey Decimal System _____

9. African country whose capital is Jeffersonia _____

10. Something a motorist can get beginning at age 14 _____

11. Assumption by animals of human form _____

12. Surgery done to increase one's weight _____

13. Invention by the Italian Ottmar Mergenthaler _____

14. Girl in Rodgers & Hammerstein's "My Fair Lady" _____

Rating   Good: 7   Excellent: 10   Ace: 13

108. SHIFTY, SHIFTY

If you shift each letter of the word PAR seven spaces down the alphabet (so A becomes H, B becomes I, C becomes J, etc.), you'll get the word WHY. Think of a word meaning "more black," which, if each of its letters is shifted seven spaces down the alphabet, will become a new word meaning "violet."

109. HOMOPHONE PAIRS

In this puzzle you're given clues for two words. Their homophones (or sound-alikes) are partners of each other in phrase.

Ex. Dove's home / Person from Bangkok

_____cote_____   _____Thai_____   [coat and tie]

1. Had on, as clothing / Part of a jigsaw puzzle

_____   _____

2. A marsh grass / Correct

_____   _____

3. Jekyll's alter ego / Member of a religious group in northern India

_____ _____

4. Kind of porridge that's "hot" in a rhyme / Lines to wait in

_____ _____

5. To stupefy / Men who are called "Sir"

_____ _____

6. Male deer / Fish that's often filleted

_____ _____

7. Complain in a high voice / Unit of force, in physics

_____ _____

8. Was victorious / Leatherworker's tool

_____ _____

9. Photo, informally / Grinds food with the teeth

_____ _____

10. Opposite of poetry / Supreme rulers of the Tatar tribes

_____ _____

11. Minty herb / Fastened with a rope

_____ _____

12. Informal word of parting / Jail compartment

_____ _____

Rating   Good: 6   Excellent: 10   Ace: 12

110. PERSONALITY CHANGES

In this puzzle you are given some made-up names of people. Change one letter in the first name and one letter in the last name to get the name of a real celebrity (past or present).

Ex. Nell Timon _Neil Simon_

1. Pansy Caine _____

2. Rocky Maltin _____

3. Bob Love _____

4. Stan Conners _____

5. Bryce Wenner _____

6. Chick Morris _____

7. Pierce Hardin _____

8. Roy Millard _____

9. Rose Peron _____

10. Ronny Bond _____

11. Willis Hays _____

12. Bart Paris _____

13. Doris Becket _____

14. Clark Burton _____

15. Nero Montel _____

Rating   Good: 8   Excellent: 12   Ace: 15

111. E FOR EFFORT

Every answer below is a familiar two-word phrase that starts and ends with the letter E.

Ex. When water flows out from the shore ___ *ebb tide* ___

1. What surrounds a yolk _____

2. Spring event when people traditionally show off new hats

_____

3. What you have to pay to compete in a contest _____

4. Strenuous physical exertion, as scrubbing _____

5. Nickname for Ireland _____

6. Nickname for New York _____

7. It carries gases away from a motor _____

8. 1.6 dollars for a pound, for example _____

9. Wisconsin city whose name is French for "clear water"

_____

10. You might pull this to bring a train to a screeching halt

_____

11. Cry in fencing _____

12. Provision that allows you to get out of a contract _____

13. Brand name for a chocolate-covered ice-cream bar

_____

14. A president might invoke it to keep secrets _____

15. It grows pine cones _____

16. Place to score a touchdown _____

Rating   Good: 9   Excellent: 13   Ace: 16

112. ALL BUT Q

Take the 25 letters of the alphabet other than Q and arrange them to spell five common, uncapitalized words. They can be any length. What are they? Hint: The initial letters of the five words are C, F, G, P, and V.

113. UNITED NATIONS

Find the name of the country hidden in each of the following sentences. Hint: Each answer is at least six letters long.

  Ex. Scientists found hid<u>den mark</u>ings.   [Denmark]

  1. The chief ran ceremonial dances.

  2. We studied algebra zillions of hours.

  3. I agree certain changes must be made.

  4. Try to find one Siamese cat.

  5. That's the best pajama I can buy.

  6. Nutritionists love niacin.

  7. The government insists on formal divestiture.

  8. Will people ban only assault rifles?

  9. That's real geriatric medicine.

  10. Find a co-star I can work with.

  11. Marty is a drug and alcohol agent.

  12. Did that skycap ever demand money?

Rating   Good: 8   Excellent: 10   Ace: 12

114. LETTER ROTATION

Each of the following sentences contains two blanks. The word that goes in the first blank contains an N somewhere in it. Rotate that N ninety degrees to form a Z to make a new word which will go in the second blank to complete the sentence.

Ex. Watching a ___*nest*___ of robins outside the window brought ___*zest*___ to the shut-in's life.

1. A sober-minded frontiersman like Daniel _____ was not known for drinking _____.

2. The emperor _____ had _____ tolerance for dissent.

3. There's such a crowd at the nightclub, you'll have to _____ your neck to see the latest dance _____.

4. A lawyer's pro _____ work requires much skill and can't be done by just any old _____.

5. French police, searching boats on the _____, were able to _____ 1,000 pounds of cocaine.

6. It's all right for a dog to take little bites at parts of your clothing, but you don't want a _____ going after your _____.

7. The early autumn frost in a state like _____ made it hard for the Indians there to grow _____.

In the final sentence, the first word contains two N's, which are both changed to Z's:

8. It's _____ how the memory tends to grow _____ over time.

Rating   Good: 4   Excellent: 6   Ace: 8

115. DEEJAYS

In this puzzle every answer is a familiar two-word phrase with the initials D-J.

Ex. Radio personality ___*disk jockey*___

1. Wrapper for a hardcover book _____

2. Second segment of a popular TV quiz show _____

3. Prominent stock average _____

4. 75th anniversary celebration _____

5. Kind of letter _____

6. Diary _____

7. Mr. Hyde's alter ego _____

8. Popular record label for rap artists _____

9. Music that New Orleans is famous for _____

10. Levi's 501's, for example _____

11. Humor involving a farmer's daughter, e.g. _____

12. Stereotypical athlete _____

13. Frame for an entrance to a room _____

14. Words following "Don't quit your …" _____

15. Great lover _____

Rating   Good: 10   Excellent: 13   Ace: 15

116. HOMOPHONIC GEOGRAPHY

Homophones are words that sound the same but are spelled differently, like OUR and HOUR. Name two countries in the world whose names can be anagrammed to get two homophones.

117. PAIR-A-GRAMS

Every answer in this puzzle is a familiar phrase in the form "___ & ___," where the words that go in the blanks have been anagrammed. What are the phrases?

Ex. MOOR & BROAD ___*room & board*___

1. NOGS & CANED _____

2. FATS & OLEOS _____

3. VEIL & RENAL _____

4. PERU & IMPELS _____

5. TRAP & PLACER _____

6. THORN & SHOUT _____

7. REGAL & MALLS _____

8. CHASE & ASPIN _____

9. ARGUS & EPICS _____

10. DOLER & WIRES _____

11. GIRTH & GROWN _____

12. HEAL & EARTHY _____

13. TAPS & SERPENT _____

14. TSARS & PERSIST _____

15. CHASER & SECURE _____

Rating   Good: 10   Excellent: 13   Ace: 15

118. LISPED INITIALS

Every answer in this puzzle is a familiar two-word phrase in which the first word starts with the letter S and the second word starts with TH.

Ex. Illness that makes it hard to talk _____ *strep throat* _____

1. Something odd sticks out like this _____

2. Reason to reconsider _____

3. Short, unspecified distance _____

4. Words before "You're out!" _____

5. What a person with a lisp might seek _____

6. Branch of mathematics involving groups of things _____

7. Former senator from South Carolina _____

8. Seasonal plays in resort communities _____

9. Weather phenomenon of March or April, after a long freeze
_____

10. It's used to stitch up a wound _____

11. One week after August 27th _____

12. 50 x 120 _____

13. Furtive burglar _____

14. Hallucinate _____

Rating   Good: 8   Excellent: 11   Ace: 14

119. TWO MORE

In this puzzle you are given two four-letter words. Put the same pair of letters after each of them to complete two familiar six-letter words. The past-tense suffix -ED is not allowed.

Ex. Tale / Flue _NT_ [talent, fluent]

1. Band / Pulp _____
2. Star / Blot _____
3. Seam / Tart _____
4. Best / Fell _____
5. Ding / Mars _____
6. Demo / Game _____
7. Stat / Tong _____
8. Doll / Hang _____
9. Flee / Pier _____
10. Bran / Come _____
11. Clot / Soot _____
12. Mode / Unto _____
13. Cave / Comb _____
14. Bull / Rock _____
15. Bush / Dies _____

Rating　　Good: 10　　Excellent: 13　　Ace: 15

120. DOWNTOWN

The phrase TALL TALE consists of two four-letter words that differ only in their last letters. Think of another familiar phrase like this—consisting of two four-letter words differing only in their last letters—that names something you might see downtown.

121. NOTHING TO IT

The answer to the first clue in each pair is a six-letter word. Add the letter O somewhere inside it to make a seven-letter word that answers the second clue.

Ex. Turkey moistener / Braggart

   baster   *boaster*

1. Place for a stoplight / One who does autopsies

   _____   _____

2. Necessity for a kite / Keeping in a warehouse

   _____   _____

3. List / Alarm on a farm

   _____   _____

4. Big box / Saturday morning TV fare

   _____   _____

5. Scheming feline from Hanna-Barbera (2 wds.) / Article of outerwear

   _____   _____

6. Go over and over, as a subject (2 wds.) / Whaler's weapon

   _____   _____

7. Person making a false signature / One who goes without

   _____   _____

8. With abruptness and rudeness / Polite

   _____   _____

9. Caped superhero / Yacht owner

   _____   _____

10. One filling positions on a film / Table protector

    _____   _____

11. Girls / Catches rodeo-style

    _____   _____

12. Instrument of the trumpet family / Small crown

    _____   _____

Rating   Good: 7   Excellent: 10   Ace: 12

122. TRIBUTE TO MISS FITZGERALD

Every answer here is a word or name that ends in -ELLA.

Ex. Guy, informally _____ *fella* _____

1. Fairy tale with a prince _____
2. Italian cheese used in pizza _____
3. Long, slender cigar _____
4. Another name for German measles _____
5. Queen who helped finance Columbus _____
6. 1968 Jane Fonda title role _____
7. Kind of policy, in insurance _____
8. Kind of poisoning _____
9. Without musical accompaniment _____
10. Kneecap _____
11. Whiplike appendages in protozoa _____
12. Parts of brains _____
13. Rapid, whirling dance _____
14. Medium-length work of fiction _____
15. Last word in "A Streetcar Named Desire" _____

Rating   Good: 10   Excellent: 13   Ace: 15

123. MANNER OF SPEAKING

Every answer in this puzzle is a familiar three-word phrase in which the middle word is "of" and the first word starts with M.

Ex. Idiom or expression _____ *manner of speaking* _____

1. Person who directs the entertainment at a party _____
2. Unmarried woman at a bride's side _____
3. Exact time when one's character is put to the test _____
4. Material for buttons and beads _____

5. Common antacid that comes in a bottle _____

6. Plus or minus number, in polling results _____

7. Something to stand on, figuratively speaking _____

8. Mammoth shopping area near Minneapolis _____

9. The boondocks _____

10. Shakespearean play, with "The" _____

11. Mozart opera _____

12. Big Z, made with a sword _____

13. Nickname for the caped crusader played by Christopher Reeve

    _____

14. Charitable organization whose goal is to eliminate birth defects

    _____

15. Philosopher's ultimate quest _____

Rating   Good: 9   Excellent: 12   Ace: 15

124. D-PLUS

If you were asked to name a familiar word that contains two S's, followed by another letter, and then two more S's, you might say ASSESSOR. What common word contains two D's, followed by another letter, and then two more D's?

125. Z-E SOUND-ALIKES

There are two blanks in each of the sentences below. The words that go in the blanks are homophones of each other—that is, they're pronounced the same but have different spellings. Hint: The word that goes in the first blank ends in the letters Z-E.

Ex. It was once common for pirates to ___*seize*___ loot on the high
___*seas*___.

1. Your palomino horses can _____ in the meadow with my dapples and _____.

2. If a police officer pulls a gun and shouts "_____!," that hardly _____ a suspect to keep running.

3. Operating a car under the influence of _____ elicits _____ from safety experts.

4. Getting conked on the head left me in a _____ for _____.

5. In a sleuthing competition, the top _____ goes to the contestant who _____ least intrusively.

6. The _____ coming through the window dried out the selection of _____ on the cheeseboard.

7. During hot summer afternoons, bucks _____ while their _____ nibble on blades of grass.

8. Grandpa, who was short of breath, let out a _____ on the roller coaster ride, amidst all the _____ from the children around him.

9. As Estelle went through clothes in the attic, seeing her old _____ six dress brought _____ of nostalgia.

10. Aunt Harriet was such an incredible stickler about telling the truth that you could practically _____ her with a _____ [3 wds.].

Rating   Good: 6   Excellent: 8   Ace: 10

126. PUBLIC ADDRESS SYSTEM

Every word below starts with the letter P. For each one think of a five-letter synonym that starts with A.

Ex. Prize ___*award*___

1. Permit _____

2. Pester _____

3. Plenty _____

4. Plus _____

5. Principle _____

6. Prevent _____

7. Prognosticate _____

8. Pointer _____

9. Perfume _____

10. Protection _____

11. Passion _____

12. Pathway _____

13. Pale _____

14. Pal _____

15. Pressing _____

16. Pend _____

17. Proficient _____

18. Pseudonym _____

Rating   Good: 11   Excellent: 15   Ace: 18

127. PREPOSITIONALLY SPEAKING

Each phrase below begins with a preposition followed by the word "the." The third word has been anagrammed. Rearrange the letters to complete a familiar phrase.

Ex. On the ONES _____nose_____

1. Under the INKS _____

2. Beside the PINTO _____

3. Behind the ITEMS _____

4. Down the NADIR _____

5. For the SOWER _____

6. From the EARTH _____

7. Off the ASCOT _____

8. To the SECURE _____

In these four-word phrases, the last two words are anagrammed. The answers are all two or more words.

9. For the GEMINI BET _____

10. In the F PARTICLES _____

11. On the NORTH HEAD _____

12. Behind the LIGHT BALE _____

13. By the NEAT SMOKE _____

14. At the FAR HOPTOAD _____

128. COUPLES ONLY

The six-letter words ACCOST, COSTAR, STARCH, ARCHER, and CHERUB overlap each other in a series as shown below:

AC CO ST AR CH ER UB

Can you form a similar chain of five other six-letter words starting with CU and ending with AL?

129. THE END OF THE BEGINNING

For each word below provide an antonym whose first letter is the same as the last letter of the word.

Ex. Small ___*large*___

1. Narrow _____

2. Short _____

3. Coming _____

4. Depth _____

5. Then _____

6. Fat _____

7. Elderly _____

8. Entrance _____

9. Minuscule _____

10. Trail _____

11. Lewd _____

12. Late _____

13. Mean _____

14. Dumb _____

15. Board _____

16. Build _____

17. Smooth _____

18. Perilous _____

19. Straight _____

20. Apart _____

Rating   Good: 13   Excellent: 17   Ace: 20

130. EXTRA POUNDS

Every answer here has five or more letters containing at least one L and one B—and no other consonants. The letter Y is not used. The lengths of the answers are provided in parentheses.

Ex. Southern girl (5) __belle__

1. Site for washing instructions (5) _____

2. Trinket (6) _____

3. "The Zoo Story" playwright (5) _____

4. One holding money for a person in jail (6) _____

5. Defamatory writing (5) _____

6. Subject to damages, at law (6) _____

7. Bubbling, as hot water (5) _____

8. Slight error, as in baseball (6) _____

9. First Spaniard to sight the Pacific Ocean (6) _____

10. Man with a secret password (3,4) _____

11. Singer Patti (7) _____

12. Talk nonsensically (6) _____

13. Like hours worked, for a lawyer (8) _____

14. Flower also called a Virginia cowslip (8) _____

15. Yale Bowl cry (5-5) _____

16. Defendant's excuse (5) _____

17. For a homeowner it goes up in the winter (3,4) _____

The last five answers include Y's among the vowels:

18. Thomas Gainsborough subject, with "The" (4,3) _____

19. Bedtime song (7) _____

20. Classic 1902 song performed by Danny Kaye and Louis Armstrong in "The Five Pennies" (4,6) _____

21. One of Paul Newman's eyes (4,4) _____

22. Character in a classic "Seinfeld" episode who lives in an artificial environment (6,3) _____

Rating   Good: 14   Excellent: 18   Ace: 21

131. R & R

Every answer here is a familiar two-word phrase in which the first word ends in R and the second word starts with R.

Ex. Something a hunter might put on his cabin floor ___*bear rug*___

1. Sign in an apartment window _____

2. A straight-A student is on it _____

3. Where athletes change clothes _____

4. Problem on a baby's bottom _____

5. Transaction at Avis or Hertz _____

6. Iowa city, home of Coe College _____

7. Item of apparel for a church singer _____

8. Electric company employee who comes around to the house _____

9. Beatrix Potter children's book character with big ears _____

10. Boxer Leonard _____

11. Focus of a political drive before an election _____

12. TV character with his own neighborhood _____

13. Government decree during a drought _____

14. Ultraconservatives _____

15. Name on an early almanac _____

16. Reason for a siren during World War II _____

Rating   Good: 12   Excellent: 14   Ace: 16

132. THE THREE B'S

What famous person's name (first and last name) is an anagram of CREATURES plus three B's?

133. WHAT OF IT?

Every answer in this puzzle is a familiar phrase in the form of "   of   ," where the first word begins with the letter C—as in "cost of living." Given the last word in the phrase, provide the first word to complete it.

    Ex. Living ___*cost*___ [cost of living]

    1. Errors _____

    2. Arms _____

    3. Whoat _____

    4. Dawn _____

    5. Worms _____

    6. Thousands _____

    7. Habit _____

    8. Duty _____

    9. Passion _____

    10. Law _____

    11. Death _____

    12. Origin _____

    13. Gold _____

    14. Silence _____

Rating   Good: 8   Excellent: 11   Ace: 14

134. ENDS FLIPPED

In this puzzle you're given the middle three letters of some familiar, uncapitalized seven-letter words. In each case the first two letters are the same as the last two letters, only reversed. Identify the words.

Ex. COV <u>recover</u>

1. STF _____

2. TWI _____

3. WSM _____

4. RPL _____

5. CAD _____

6. TEN _____

7. POU _____

8. RDI _____

9. OUG _____

10. DEN _____

11. GWO _____

12. RNO _____

Rating Good: 5 Excellent: 9 Ace: 12

135. SHE'S BACK!

For each five-letter girl's name below, think of a word that contains its letters spelled consecutively backward. Some of the names have more than one possible answer.

Ex. MARGE <u>TELEGRAM</u>

1. DELLA _____

2. TATUM _____

3. IRENE _____

4. RENEE _____

5. SARAH _____

6. ILONA _____

7. MELBA _____

8. AGNES _____

9. TERRI _____

10. MEGAN _____

Rating   Good: 5   Excellent: 8   Ace: 10

136. TO SURVIVE ... OR FAIL

What familiar two-word phrase means both "to help to survive" and "to give up in failure"? The first phrase is informal, and the second is slang.

137. WHO'S THAT SINGING?

The names of some famous singers are listed below, but in each case the singer's last name has been replaced with an anagram. Unscramble the letters to name the singer.

Ex. Frank ARTISAN __*Sinatra*__

1. Elvis YELPERS _____

2. Julie WANDERS _____

3. Josephine BREAK _____

4. Ray CLASHER _____

5. Vic MOANED _____

6. Bobby NADIR _____

7. Lena HERON _____

8. Kenny GOSLING _____

9. Charley REDIP _____

10. John BASSANITE _____

11. Dinah HORSE _____

12. Rod SWATTER _____

13. Mel MÉTRO _____

14. LeAnn MISER _____

15. George ARTIST _____

16. Barbra TARDINESS _____

138. DOUBLE-A

Every answer below is a familiar two-word phrase in which both words have one syllable with a long-A vowel sound.

Ex. To cause a disturbance ___*raise Cain*___

1. It's hard to keep this while telling a silly joke _____

2. It carries heavy goods by rail _____

3. It officially began with the launch of Sputnik _____

4. Backup time for a postponed game _____

5. Large, short-haired dog _____

6. Flexible armor _____

7. Kleenex or Coca-Cola, e.g. _____

8. Common money-raising event for a women's group _____

9. Opposite of a dieting effect _____

10. Length of time for "a week" in a Beatles hit _____

11. Nickname for Massachusetts _____

12. Any member of the Confederacy, until 1865 _____

13. Slow rate of moving _____

14. Electrical impulses given off by the head _____

139. THREE TO ONE

Each of the following sentences has two blanks. Switch the first and third letters of the word that goes in either blank to get the other.

Ex. When her manufacturer's ___*rebate*___ didn't arrive fast enough, the customer called to ___*berate*___ company officials.

1. My wisecracking grandma, sitting in her _____, told a _____ of a joke.

2. Hurry up! Don't _____ if you want to see the duck _____ across the road.

3. After Fort _____ was fired upon at the start of the Civil War, Confederate officials worked to _____ support for their cause.

4. Anyone who commits a crime in Katmandu will experience the harsh _____ system of _____.

5. In India, a can of tomato _____ costs just one _____.

6. After coming indoors from mowing the lawn, I had to _____ my steps across the _____ to get back out to the mower.

7. The biochemist raced to find a cure for a _____ infection before his bitter _____.

8. Every 5,280 feet, we passed a _____ on the long road to the _____ quarry.

9. Cleaning up the water along the Maine coast should _____ the _____ production for fishermen.

10. The fruit stand was stocked with both _____ and _____.

Rating   Good: 5   Excellent: 8   Ace: 10

140. LET'S BE REALISTIC

What familiar phrase meaning "is realistic" consists of two words that are exactly the same except for their fourth letters? The length of these two words is for you to determine.

141. HOW ODD!

In this puzzle you're given some four-letter words. They comprise the letters in the odd positions (that is, the first, third, fifth, and seventh letters) of some familiar seven-letter words. You supply the letters in the even positions to complete the words.

Ex. ACRE __*accurse*__

1. BANK _____

2. BRAN _____

3. CAKE _____

4. CLUE _____

5. CUBE _____

6. FROG _____

7. GLEN _____

8. LOAD _____

9. PROM _____

10. ROBS _____

11. SILT _____

12. SNAP _____

13. SPOT _____

14. TERM _____

15. TRUE _____

Rating Good: 7   Excellent: 11   Ace: 15

142. READY? ACTION!

In each line below, what verb can precede each of the two things named in two different senses?

    Ex. A furnace / An incompetent employee __*fire*__
        [you fire a furnace and you fire an incompetent employee]

1. An eyelash / A baseball _____

2. An envelope / Your foot _____

3. Someone's shoulder / A telephone _____

4. Vegetables / An incompetent employee _____

5. A lollipop / A child that deserves punishing _____

6. The outdoor scenery in a film / A bad film _____

7. An unpleasant interruption / Your P's and Q's _____

8. Bubbles / An easy shot, if you're nervous _____

9. A personal note / Wandering sheep _____

In the last group, the same verb applies to all three things:

10. An eggshell / A smile / A joke _____

11. A picture / A conclusion / Straws _____

12. A movie / A fishing line / Aspersions _____

Rating   Good: 7   Excellent: 10   Ace: 12

143. BY THE DOZEN

In each of the following equations, starting with the number 12, identify what the initials stand for.

Ex. 12 = I. on a R. _Inches on a Ruler_

1. 12 = M. in a Y. _____

2. 12 = S. of the Z. _____

3. 12 = D. of C. _____

4. 12 = A. (of J.C.) _____

5. 12 = E. in a C. _____

6. 12 = M. of a J. _____

7. 12 = P. on a C.F.T. _____

8. 12 = H. on the F. of a C. _____

Rating   Good: 3   Excellent: 5   Ace: 7

144. SOU'WESTER

The letters in UNGOODLY can be rearranged to spell YOUNG and OLD—which go together to make the phrase "young and old." What other familiar phrase in the form "___ and ___" has two words that can be spelled from SOU'WESTER?

145. T FOR TWO

Each sentence below contains two blanks. The word that goes in the first blank contains a T in it somewhere. Change that T to a TH and the result, phonetically, will be a new word that goes in the second blank to complete the sentence.

Ex. In philosophy class, students are ___taught___ the history of Western ___thought___ .

1. Our family is visiting _____ McHenry this _____ of July.

2. Barbara confirmed that she was dumping her boyfriend when she told him, "It's _____, we're _____."

3. Now that you can get a _____ of gas for under $20, you should be very _____.

4. Alas, what a _____ it is that the long-winded writer isn't more _____.

5. The _____ of the tire was so worn away that you could see many a _____ underneath.

6. Because the garlic _____ had such horrible breath, the dentist wanted to take _____ himself before extracting the man's tooth.

7. All you could see was the cowboy's _____ protruding from the open telephone _____.

8. If a poisonous snake strikes your knee, _____ a tourniquet around your _____.

9. Despite hours spent sifting _____ at the archeological dig, unlucky researchers found a _____ of relics.

10. Since Mrs. Shakespeare adored receding hairlines, Will threw his _____ [2 wds.] for Anne _____.

Rating   Good: 5   Excellent: 8   Ace: 10

146. THE NAME RINGS A BELL

In the two-word phrases below, each word rhymes with the first and last names respectively of a famous person past or present. Who is it?

Ex. Strike three ___*Spike Lee*___

1. Snack bar _____

2. Get smart _____

3. Loan givers _____

4. Spruce tree _____

5. Place kick _____

6. Dirt pile _____

7. Mess hall _____

8. Tan line _____

9. Fan jets _____

10. Mule skinner _____

11. Plain diet _____

12. Weight loss _____

Rating   Good: 6   Excellent: 9   Ace: 12

147. HIDDEN MYTHOLOGY

Each sentence below conceals a name from Greek or Roman mythology. Who is it? Hint: Every answer has six or more letters.

    Ex. Dad eats a turnip. [Saturn]

1. Take another message.

2. The examiner validated our claim.

3. The incumbent leads in a poll out today.

4. That is one exposé I don't want to read!

5. We flew to Africa, then Asia.

6. A smart emissary keeps quiet.

7. Jane married an inept, uneducated boor.

8. Can you see a dinosaur or anything?

9. The caribou ran usually about two hours a day.

10. A good gardener keeps a sharp hoe busy.

11. Let's disperse phones throughout the house.

12. Nothing can top Rome, the U.S.A., or Paris for a honeymoon.

Rating   Good: 8   Excellent: 10   Ace: 12

148. GIRL TO BOY

Think of a certain two-syllable girl's name in which the first vowel is I. Change the I to a U and you'll get a common boy's name in one syllable. What is it?

149. D'OH!

Every answer here is a solid word that ends in the syllable "doh" (spelled D-O).

    Ex. Philosophy to live by ___credo___

    1. Denver's state _____

    2. City sometimes called "holy" _____

    3. Twister _____

    4. Expert or devotee _____

    5. Gilbert and Sullivan classic, with "The" _____

    6. Fruit also known as an alligator pear _____

    7. Common name for a dog _____

    8. Means of self-defense _____

    9. In music, a gradual increase in loudness _____

    10. Suit worn at a wedding _____

    11. Boasting _____

    12. Indirect disparagement or criticism _____

    13. Antiterrorist fighter, for example _____

    14. Ornery outlaw _____

    15. The "T" of PT boat _____

    16. Cadillac model named after a legendary city _____

    17. Sex drive _____

    18. Dummy _____

Rating   Good: 11   Excellent: 15   Ace: 18

150. LOSING IT

The answer to the first clue in each pair below contains the consecutive letters I-T somewhere inside. Remove the I-T, and you'll get a new word that answers the second clue.

    Ex. Well-mannered / Resident of Warsaw ___polite___ [Pole]

    1. Where London is / Where the cerebellum is _____

2. To stir up / Certain marble _____

3. To bleach / Reporter's question _____

4. Subject for Sir Isaac Newton / Thanksgiving serving _____

5. A guest / An eyeshade _____

6. Mexican sandwich / Pack animal _____

7. Letters that look like football goalposts / Hurts _____

8. Speed / Stalk at a salad bar _____

9. Police artist's drawing of a suspect / To write music _____

10. "The White Whale" for "Moby Dick" / Understated _____

Rating   Good: 5   Excellent: 8   Ace: 10

151. FORE-AND-AFT RHYMES

In this puzzle you're given two words that rhyme. For each pair think of a third word that can follow each of the given words to complete a compound word or a familiar two-word phrase. The lengths of the answers are provided in parentheses.

Ex. Wish, Fish (4) ____**bone**____ [wishbone, fish bone]

1. Early, Whirly (4) _____

2. Pool, School (4) _____

3. Band, Grand (5) _____

4. Fair, Stair (3) _____

5. Fare, Stair (4) _____

6. Knot, Pot (4) _____

7. View, Dew (5) _____

8. Cue, Screw (4) _____

9. Jack, Crack (3) _____

10. Post, Toast (6) _____

11. High, Sky (5) _____

12. Floor, Score (5) _____

13. Roll, Toll (4) _____

14. Man, Pan (6) _____

In the last example, think of a word that can follow each of the three given words:

    15. Dead, Head, Bread (4) _____

Rating   Good: 8   Excellent: 12   Ace: 15

152. HALF OFF

Think of a certain six-letter word. Drop its first three letters. Shift each of the remaining letters one space down the alphabet (that is, A would become B, B would become C, etc.), and the result will be a word that means the opposite of the original. What is it? Hint: Both the six-letter word and the final three-letter word start with the same letter of the alphabet.

153. OH! OH!

In this puzzle every answer is a familiar two-word phrase in which each word has one syllable and the vowel sound in that syllable is a long O.

    Ex. Old-fashioned heating device ____*coal stove*____

    1. The front of a rocket _____

    2. New Year's Day event _____

    3. You have to pay to drive on it _____

    4. What E.T. was supposed to do _____

    5. Oscar Hammerstein musical with the song "Can't Help Lovin' Dat Man" _____

    6. It's represented by an open ring on a musical staff _____

    7. To become bankrupt _____

    8. Lorillard cigarette brand _____

    9. Slang for a bald person _____

    10. Nay, in the Senate _____

    11. What footballs are kicked through _____

    12. Object that's turned upside-down and shaken _____

    13. Grain product that's a major ingredient of granola _____

    14. Punctuation mark that looks like two apostrophes, used mainly at the end of a sentence _____

Rating   Good: 9   Excellent: 12   Ace: 14

154. SMALL DIFFERENCE

Change just one letter in each of the following sentences so as to completely reverse its meaning.

Ex. The guard will not let you through the gate. _____ *now* _____

1. The steel company plans to hire five thousand more workers.
_____

2. The 79-year-old man is in weak physical condition. _____

3. The moon will be waxing for the next seven days. _____

4. In matters of romance, something the suitor did could be described as "class." _____

5. The canvas hanging in the modern art museum was completely blank.
_____

6. All you'll need is your brain to solve this series of challenges.
_____

7. Authorities had the border tightly controlled. _____

8. The police chief is backing the mayor's orders. _____

9. Jack was surprised to find his blind date so homely. _____

10. All the critics spoke avidly about the new film. _____

11. The appellate brief was supported by none of the Supreme Court justices.
_____

12. After investing $50,000 in her store, Margaret's business is sailing.
_____

13. American troops arrived and gave the Japanese help. _____

14. Winds were mild for our whole vacation. _____

15. The House member was elected by an overwhelming majority last November. _____

Rating   Good: 11   Excellent: 13   Ace: 15

155. POSTSCRIPT

In this puzzle every answer is a compound word in which the first part ends in P and the last part starts with S.

Ex. Attire for a parachutist _____ *jumpsuit* _____

1. Something you can check your oil with _____

2. Children's game played on a sidewalk _____

3. Insignificant person _____

4. Logger's tool _____

5. Bird sometimes called "yellow-bellied" _____

6. Something that might be put on a tennis ball _____

7. Where to pitch a tent _____

8. Standard item in a woman's purse _____

9. Slang for "to throw away" _____

10. Three Stooges humor _____

11. Implement for eating a Campbell's product _____

12. Boy who is a relation by marriage _____

13. Tightwad _____

14. Diploma _____

15. Publishers Clearing House contest _____

Rating   Good: 10   Excellent: 13   Ace: 15

156. HEAD-TO-TAIL SHIFT

Think of a certain word starting with the letter E. Move the E to the end, and the result will be the names of two animals side by side. What are they? Hint: The first animal is fairly large, and the second one is small.

157. IF IT'S ALL THE SAME TO YOU

Rearrange the letters in each pair of words below to get two homophones—that is, words that are pronounced the same but spelled differently.

Ex. WORDS _SWORD_   ADORES _SOARED_

1. KEEP _____   EQUIP _____

2. ORGAN _____   WRONG _____

3. TIRE _____   GIRTH _____

4. RASPY _____	ASPIRE _____
5. WAITS _____	SWEAT _____
6. DOWER _____	REDO _____
7. RAIL _____	RELY _____
8. SEALED _____	SLATE _____
9. NAKED _____	EDEN _____
10. CASHED _____	SCATHE _____
11. SANEST _____	STANCE _____
12. STRUT _____	DUSTERS _____

Rating   Good: 8   Excellent: 10   Ace: 12

158. 150 WORDS

If you write the lowercase letters "c" and "l" together, they look like a "d." In this puzzle you're given clues for two words. The first word starts with the letters "c-l." Change the "c-l" to a "d," and you'll get the second word.

Ex. Spotless / College official __*clean*__   [dean]

1. Timekeeper / Landing pier _____

2. Kitchen spice / Bird of peace _____

3. Sound of a barnyard fowl / Barnyard fowl _____

4. Sticking to the body / Dull and drab _____

5. Automobile control / One way to "go" on a date _____

6. Become silent (2 wds.) / Block (2 wds.) _____

7. Tongue of a bell / Neatly dressed _____

8. What a quiz-game player holds / To bargain _____

9. Bunch / Maid's implement _____

10. Not going well together, as colors / Lively _____

11. Fast-moving ship / Ladle _____

12. Woman's name / Another woman's name _____

Rating   Good: 7   Excellent: 10   Ace: 12

159. WHAT THE H—?

Each sentence below has two blanks. Add an H to the end of the word that goes in the first blank to get a new word that goes in the second blank to complete the sentence.

Ex. The lazy student lost her _____slot_____ on the dean's schedule because of her unfortunate _____sloth_____.

1. The big circus _____ goes up on June _____.

2. In trying to _____ a horn last New Year's Eve, Brian chipped a _____.

3. In the 1960s, burning their _____ was a _____ thing for women to do.

4. The producers of "All in the Family" wanted to _____ out a comment by _____ Bunker.

5. Your telescopic view of _____ may be obscured tonight by the rising _____ gases.

6. You can win a genuine leather cowboy _____ in the next carnival _____.

7. The carpet is a beautiful red, _____ its pile is wonderfully _____!

8. Mel _____ began to _____ when he heard the embarrassing mistake he had made voicing Porky Pig.

9. The French churchgoers had to travel to _____ to find a new _____ priest.

10. On Valentine's Day mother hung a giant red _____ above the stone _____.

Rating Good: 5   Excellent: 8   Ace: 10

160. REACHING THE SAME CONCLUSION

A certain famous woman has five letters in both her first and last names—and the last three letters of her first name are the same as the last three letters of her last name, in the same order. Who is she?

161. AND WHAT?

This puzzle features phrases in the form "___ & ___," where the last word starts with the letter D. Given the first word, complete each phrase.

Ex. Hill ___dale___ [hill & dale]

1. Five _____
2. Wheel _____
3. Wine _____
4. Gloom _____
5. Ups _____
6. Life _____
7. Mom _____
8. Song _____
9. Fine _____
10. Near _____
11. Car _____
12. Night _____
13. High _____
14. Cloak _____
15. Hopes _____
16. Down _____
17. Dots _____
18. Cut _____
19. Bound _____
20. Cease _____
21. Search _____
22. Dungeons _____
23. Stand _____
24. Supply _____

Rating   Good: 17   Excellent: 21   Ace: 24

162. SIMPLE AS A, B, C

Given three words beginning with the letters A, B, and C, provide a fourth word that can follow each of the others to complete a compound word or a familiar two-word phrase.

Ex. Apple, Black, Car __*jack*__ [applejack, blackjack, carjack]

1. Asteroid, Bible, Conveyor _____
2. Alley, Bob, Copy _____
3. Assembly, Border, Clothes _____
4. Armored, Box, Cable _____
5. Artillery, Band, Clam _____
6. Address, Bank, Cook _____
7. Above, Base, Clip _____
8. Arrow, Block, Copper _____
9. American, Big, Cream _____
10. Altar, Bell, Cow _____
11. Attack, Bull, Corn _____
12. Ankle, Back, Crazy _____
13. Atomic, Binary, Call _____
14. Antitrust, Bathing, Civil _____

Rating   Good: 7   Excellent: 11   Ace: 14

163. SUDDENLY SINGLE

The following sentences each have two blanks. The word that goes in the first blank has a doubled T somewhere in it. Change it to a single T to get a new word that goes in the second blank to complete the sentence.

Ex. "Think fast" was the unofficial ___*motto*___ of Japanese detective Mr. ___*Moto*___.

1. Drinking a _____ at the coffee shop this morning made me _____ for work.

2. The newborn _____ of puppies drank almost a _____ of milk.

3. To make a successful golf _____, you have to _____ just the right amount of force into the shot.

4. The Idaho company's plans were left in _____ after its _____ were pulled from grocery shelves nationwide.

5. The woman chose a _____ finish for the paint on her bedroom walls because her _____ didn't want a sheen.

6. Because the office busybody was always _____ on her co-workers, she got a low _____ for employee relations from her boss.

7. Since the pet store customer had specifically requested a dog that was safe for kids, he was _____ about having been stuck with a _____.

8. I do not care one _____ what _____ the publisher gives my book.

9. The Pakistani nuclear official would not _____ to the fact that it had just conducted another _____ [hyph. wd.].

Rating   Good: 5   Excellent: 7   Ace: 9

164. F TROOP

Think of a certain six-letter word starting with F. Move the F from the first position to the fourth position and you'll get a new word that means the opposite of the original. What is it? Hint: The second word is hyphenated.

165. MMM ...

To each word below, add two or more M's (as shown) and rearrange all the letters to make a new word.

    Ex. BEER + MM   <u>MEMBER</u>

    1. YORE + MM _____

    2. BLUE + MM _____

    3. YEAH + MM _____

    4. RAYS + MM _____

    5. RUSE + MM _____

    6. AIRED + MM _____

    7. LIKEN + MM _____

8. ARGUE + MM _____

9. TOPSY + MM _____

10. AILED + MM _____

11. SEINE + MM _____

12. OATH + MMM _____

13. SERIES + MMM _____

14. RONDEAU + MMM _____

15. AGORA + MMMM _____

Rating   Good: 8   Excellent: 12   Ace: 15

166. JUST FOR YOU

Every answer here is a word or name that begins with the syllable "you" (in any spelling).

Ex. River through Iraq __*Euphrates*__

1. Hawaiian musical instrument _____

2. Card game played with a 32-card deck _____

3. Site of an 1898 gold rush _____

4. One-of-a-kind _____

5. In every place _____

6. Tree with chewable leaves _____

7. Big film studio _____

8. Mexican peninsula _____

9. Hero of the "Odyssey" _____

10. Shangri-la _____

11. Speech at a funeral _____

12. Any tool _____

13. Exorbitant interest rates _____

14. Classic name in geometry _____

15. Mythical animal _____

16. Extreme happiness _____

17. Its capital is Kampala _____

18. Country bordering Romania [two answers] _____
_____

Rating   Good: 12   Excellent: 15   Ace: 18

167. HIDDEN COMPOSERS

Each of the following sentences conceals the name of a famous composer in left-to-right order. Who is it?

Ex. The other berth is higher.   [Victor Herbert]

1. Grab a chair.

2. Never dillydally.

3. Is Eric hoping to win?

4. His survival didn't last long.

5. Put the church bell in its steeple.

6. Legislators called the tobacco plan "dead."

7. His chum annoys me.

8. Two cities include bus systems in their plans.

9. Play some other game, not tiddlywinks.

10. Please label garments correctly.

11. The twins finished tenth and eleventh.

12. What is Carl attired in?

Rating   Good: 8   Excellent: 10   Ace: 12

168. BODY LANGUAGE

Think of two particular parts of the body in three and four letters, respectively. Insert the three-letter word exactly in the middle of the four-letter word, and the result will name something that's sometimes found on top of a building. What is it?

169. HINKITY-PINKITY

This puzzle is a game of "Hinkity-Pinkity," where every answer is a pair of three-syllable words that rhyme.

Ex. Devotion to a king or queen ___royalty loyalty___

1. Less noisy member of a mob _____

2. Things that cured a famous inventor's illnesses _____

3. Vows made by President Jefferson _____

4. President Taylor's rum cocktails _____

5. How-to book that comes out once a year _____

6. Less kind diamond seller _____

7. Improving one's printing _____

8. Certain gas stations south of the Rio Grande _____

9. Harshly criticize a 1990s first lady _____

10. Current White House occupant _____

11. A drawing for ceramic ware _____

12. Boredom for a séance leader _____

13. Stonehenge, Amelia Earhart's disappearance, etc. _____

14. People that a magazine worker owes money to _____

15. One who totes obstructions _____

16. Craftsperson who takes political sides _____

17. Service club's cliques _____

18. Elastic plants seen around a yard _____

Rating   Good: 11   Excellent: 15   Ace: 18

170. TWO L'S

Every answer in this puzzle is a compound or hyphenated word in which each half begins with the letter L.

Ex. Rope that you throw to a person who's drowning ___lifeline___

1. Kind of binder _____

2. Insect known as "daddy" _____

3. People with romance problems _____

4. Like Bolivia, Switzerland, or Nepal _____

5. Flavor of Sprite _____

6. Cowardly _____

7. Dull or without flair _____

8. Person who is paid rent _____

9. Epithet for undesirable people _____

10. Host Art of 1950s-'60s afternoon TV _____

11. The center of public attention or notoriety _____

12. Person who doesn't know much about sailing _____

Rating Good: 7   Excellent: 10   Ace: 12

171. BB'S

For each word below, add two B's and rearrange all the letters to spell a new word.

Ex. LIE + BB _BIBLE_

1. IRE + BB _____

2. AIR + BB

3. OAT + BB

4. POE + BB _____

5. TACO + BB _____

6. LOGE + BB _____

7. OH NO + BB _____

8. IRON + BB _____

9. HAYS + BB _____

10. SOAR + BB _____

11. REALM + BB _____

12. DOLES + BB _____

13. ATOMS + BB _____

14. LOYAL + BB _____

15. AGENA + BB _____

Rating Good: 8   Excellent: 12   Ace: 15

172. BRONTE'S LETTERS

Take the name BRONTE. Can you use these six letters, repeating them as often as necessary, to spell a familiar 13-letter phrase?

173. CB TALK

Every answer in this puzzle is a familiar two-word phrase with the initials C-B.

Ex. Snickers or 3 Musketeers, e.g. ___*candy bar*___

1. What a seer gazes into _____

2. Thief who climbs in upstairs windows _____

3. Unconditional permission _____

4. Soft-drink containers that thick glasses are often compared to _____

5. Game for Charles Goren or Omar Sharif _____

6. Short rest from office work _____

7. Young male attendant on a ship _____

8. "Superman" or "Archie," e.g. _____

9. French term for a distinguished chef _____

10. What a chef slices meat on _____

11. Irish dish often served with cabbage _____

12. Common ingredient in suntan lotion _____

13. Longtime quiz program sponsored by G.E _____

14. Inability to perceive certain hues _____

15. Things your mother wears, in a classic putdown _____

16. Firm that rates your ability to pay debts _____

17. Area just behind home plate _____

18. Coffee and a roll, say, in the morning _____

Rating   Good: 11   Excellent: 15   Ace: 18

174. MUTUAL REPLACEMENTS

Each of the six-letter words below has a letter repeated—not necessarily
consecutively. Change that letter to another letter in the word, and change that other
letter to the one that was repeated. The result will be a new six-letter word.

    Ex. SUNNED   _sudden_   [the two N's become D's, and the D becomes an N]

    1. LETTER _____

    2. MADDEN _____

    3. TITLED _____

    4. CORRAL _____

    5. BOGGLE _____

    6. FETTER _____

    7. RAMONA _____

    8. DAPPLE _____

    9. TILLER _____

  10. ARREST _____

  11. REDOES _____

  12. Use your answer from #11 to make another word in the same way
    _____

Rating   Good: 7   Excellent: 10   Ace: 12

175. DOUBLING BACK

The answer to the first clue in each pair has five letters. Double the middle letter and
then reverse everything to get a six-letter word that answers the second clue.

    Ex. Remove stickiness from / Held up at gunpoint

        degum   _mugged_

    1. Part of the arm that bends / Move unsteadily

        _____   _____

    2. Dieter's lunch / Second-largest city in Texas

        _____   _____

    3. Dishes with lots of ingredients / Chocolates

        _____   _____

4. Daughter of King Lear / Shrew

   _____   _____

5. Railroad station / Exceeded

   _____   _____

6. Someone who can take a joke / Soldiers

   _____   _____

7. Famous "Uncle" / Vacation time

   _____   _____

8. French impressionist known for painting ballet dancers / Drooped

   _____   _____

9. Part of the head that may be congested / Some Muslims

   _____   _____

10. Raring to go / Popular form of music from Jamaica

   _____   _____

Rating   Good: 5   Excellent: 8   Ace: 10

176. TWO TREES

Start with the letter B, add the name of a tree, then add the letter D, and finally add the name of another tree. The result will be a word that you might say when trying to solve this puzzle. What is it?

177. TAKING OFF THE CURVES

The answer to the first clue in each pair has a doubled S somewhere in it. Remove both S's and you'll get a new word that answers the second clue.

   Ex. Full of chutzpah / Donkey's sound ___*brassy*___ [bray]

   1. Archeological remnant of a dinosaur / Food wrapping material

      _____

   2. Giving orders / Sound of a spring _____

   3. To have / Group assisting a sheriff _____

   4. Ropes at a rodeo / Country in Southeast Asia _____

   5. Stylish and elegant / Modeler's material _____

6. Unnecessary / Something that has just one eye _____

7. Puddinglike dessert / Pouting grimace _____

8. Sacred or holy / To run, as a color _____

9. Risqué quality / City in Wisconsin _____

10. One who strokes lovingly / Profession _____

11. Ability to kill / Writer's due date _____

12. Flower / Flower _____

Rating   Good: 6   Excellent: 9   Ace: 12

178. ADD-ONS

Each of the following sentences has two blanks. Add -EY at the end of the word that goes in the first blank to get a new word that goes in the second blank to complete the sentence.

Ex. The young Benedictine _____**monk**_____ was as agile as a _____**monkey**_____.

1. Two things I wanted after being arrested: $500 _____ and a phone call to F. Lee _____.

2. The alcoholic janitor momentarily put down his _____ broom and took a swig of _____.

3. After Clem the _____ kissed his girlfriend too hard on the neck, she tried to hide her _____ from her parents.

4. If you'll _____ hard on this rope, the _____ will help you lift the 200-pound weight.

5. It seemed to _____ the slave Octavius to have to pull oars all day in a _____.

6. A _____ living under a bridge might see a _____ pass regularly overhead.

7. The athlete was in _____ up to his ears after spending a thousand dollars on _____ equipment.

8. The store required _____ deliveries to be made via the _____.

9. Hitting a golf ball into a soggy _____ by the ninth hole caused Humphrey to get a _____.

10. The young girl came out of her _____ when she started reading romantic poets like _____.

Rating   Good: 5   Excellent: 8   Ace: 10

179. NEW TESTAMENT

Every answer in this puzzle is a word in which the only consonants are N and T, repeated as often as necessary. Hint: Y's are not used. The lengths of the answers are provided in parentheses.

Ex. Idea (6) __*notion*__

1. Make tidy (6) _____

2. College student's cost (7) _____

3. France or China, for example (6) _____

4. Understanding between countries (7) _____

5. Aerial (7) _____

6. A number to hold on in blackjack (8) _____

7. Purpose, or what you mean to do (9) _____

8. Actor Banderas (7) _____

9. Apartment dweller (6) _____

10. Vehemently on management's side in a strike (9) _____

11. Bit of writing in the margin of a book (10) _____

12. Gut feeling (9) _____

13. Manner of speaking (10) _____

14. Very long, as odds (3-2-3) _____

15. Neglectfulness, daydreaming (11) _____

16. Marie who was married to Louis XVI (10) _____

Rating   Good: 8   Excellent: 12   Ace: 15

180. LONG GONE

Think of a certain five-letter word meaning "useful." Now think of another five-letter word meaning "dirty." Put them one after the other, and the result will spell the name of something that has not existed for more than 1,500 years. What is it?

181. HIGH SCHOOL LANGUAGE

Every answer below is a familiar two-word phrase with the initials H-S.

Ex. Colorful article of apparel __Hawaiian shirt__

1. Someone who gets A's in school _____
2. Where to have a permanent done _____
3. Where to buy hammers, nails, etc. _____
4. Social elite _____
5. TV game show based on tic-tac-toe _____
6. Deli item often made with rye bread _____
7. What a luau dancer wears _____
8. Nickname for Indiana _____
9. Event for an equestrian _____
10. It may be put on food and makes the mouth burn _____
11. Piece of equipment for an athlete on skates _____
12. Faster's protest _____
13. Initial advantage in a race _____
14. Part of a race before the finish line _____
15. Wow! (as heard on "Batman") _____

Rating   Good: 9   Excellent: 12   Ace: 15

182. APPENDAGES

Each sentence below has two blanks. The word that goes in the first blank has four letters. Add A-G-E at the end of it to get a new word that goes in the second blank to complete the sentence.

Ex. After the two-hour ___Mass___ at church, Terry went home to a nice relaxing ___massage___.

1. There are a _____ of reasons why you wouldn't want to be taken _____ at a bank robbery.

2. When the rock _____ started smashing their instruments, one member needed a _____ for a cut he suffered.

3. A boastful person will always _____ that he is above _____ in everything he does.

4. A stunning picture of _____ Blanc appears in a photo _____ on my wall.

5. When the fruit on the _____ tree was ripe, birds with beautiful _____ came to eat it.

6. As rumor spread that only one Viagra _____ remained in the town pharmacy, several dozen men tried to _____ the place.

7. After the _____ to the courthouse was not completed on time, angry advocates for the disabled went on a _____.

8. "Clean up the _____ in your room!" was the clear and unmistakable _____ from mom.

9. Near the _____ of the hill, the news crew got some stunning _____ of the car crash.

10. A future James _____ film has the hero captured by Somali warlords and sold into _____.

Rating   Good: 6   Excellent: 8   Ace: 10

183. PJ'S

Every answer in this puzzle is a familiar two-word phrase with the initials P-J.

Ex. Purple-colored preserves _____ plum jelly _____

1. Ordinary-looking girl _____

2. Container for gherkins _____

3. Whoopee cushion or exploding cigar _____

4. 1950s-'60s Vatican leader _____

5. It's when someone gets what they deserve _____

6. Seattle-based rock group led by Eddie Vedder _____

7. Beverage that helps improve your regularity _____

8. Sailor's coat _____

9. A refinish on a car _____

10. 1940 Rodgers & Hart musical starring Gene Kelly _____

11. 1960s sitcom set in Hooterville _____

12. Informally, a place to get a dish with sausage & mushroom

_____

Rating   Good: 6   Excellent: 9   Ace: 12

184. SOMETHING IN COMMON

What unusual property do the following three words have in common?

FLOUR
TERN
THIRSTY

185. WHAT'S DOING?

In this puzzle you are given three words. Supply another word that can precede each of these to complete a compound word or a familiar two-word phrase. Hint: Each answer has two syllables and ends in I-N-G.

Ex. Streak, Smile, Ticket ___*winning*___
     [winning streak, winning smile, winning ticket]

1. Jacks, Bean, Jehoshaphat _____
2. Gallery, Star, Match _____
3. Beauty, Bag, Sickness _____
4. Saucer, Carpet, Squirrel _____
5. Class, Order, Girl _____
6. Pretty, Duck, Bull _____
7. Joke, Start, Board _____
8. Range, Rain, School _____
9. Parts, Van, Target _____
10. Chance, Mad, Irish _____
11. Pin, Hills, Stones _____
12. Grade, Fancy, Lane _____
13. Card, Field, Favorites _____
14. Stock, Gas, Hyena _____

Rating   Good: 9   Excellent: 12   Ace: 14

186. PH SYSTEM

Every answer here is a familiar two-word phrase or name with the initials P-H.

Ex. Place to play billiards ____pool hall____

1. Something made of straw to wear on the head _____

2. Headgear for a safari _____

3. Work animal in a farmer's field _____

4. A substitute in the batting lineup _____

5. Full house or royal flush, e.g. _____

6. He said "Give me liberty, or give me death" _____

7. It was bombed on December 7, 1941 _____

8. Military decoration _____

9. Apartment buildings owned by the government _____

10. New York City landmark, locale of Kay Thompson's "Eloise" books
_____

11. 1960's group with the hit "A Whiter Shade of Pale" _____

12. 1985 comedy about a Mafia family, for which Anjelica Huston won an Oscar _____

13. Warner Books or Simon & Schuster _____

14. Rival of Domino's in the fast-food business _____

15. Slang for someone who's always trying to get his name in the papers
_____

Rating   Good: 10   Excellent: 13   Ace: 15

187. TURNING HEADS

Each answer in this puzzle is a phrase of three four-letter words that are all the same except for the first letter in each word.

Ex. Keep frigid fungus ____hold cold mold____

1. Identical title arrived _____

2. Genuine calves' meat dinner _____

3. Mailed a lady's partner apartment money _____

4. New Haven college man with ashen skin _____

5. A desire for filet of sole, for instance _____

6. Glass containers for certain chocolate candy _____

7. Go for a long walk in the style of boxer Tyson _____

The following answers all have four words:

8. An extended tune about a former British colony _____

9. Describe a certain brand of cigarettes as having unusual height

_____

10. Congress is going to vote down a proposed law _____

Rating   Good: 5   Excellent: 8   Ace: 10

188. SADIST'S UNDOING

The word SADIST has four consonants—S, D, S, and T, in that order—reading from left to right. Can you think of a familiar phrase in 10 letters that has only these four consonants, in the same order, reading from left to right? That is, add six vowels to S-D-S-T to make a familiar phrase in 10 letters.

189. THICKET OF TREES

They say "you can't see the forest for the trees." Well, in this puzzle we'll find out if you can see the trees! Each of the words below conceals the name of a variety of tree in left to right order—although not in consecutive letters. Every answer has five or more letters.

Ex. CHEDDAR ___cedar___

1. MAYPOLE _____

2. BESMIRCH _____

3. PERCHANCE _____

4. COLLUSIVE _____

5. PRELAUNCH _____

6. POPULAR _____

7. BLOCKBUSTER _____

8. SHORTCHANGE _____

9. WILDFLOWER _____

10. PLEASURELESS _____

11. MISPRONOUNCE _____

12. APPLAUDER [two answers] _____ _____

Rating   Good: 6   Excellent: 10   Ace: 13 (including both parts of #12)

190. MAKING GUESSES

Every answer in this puzzle is a familiar two-word phrase in which the first word ends in -ING and the second word starts with G.

Ex. Where high-speed cars are tested ___*proving ground*___

1. What pugilists wear on their hands _____

2. What a bride wears _____

3. Wrigley's product _____

4. A, B, C, or D, but not F _____

5. City in Ohio, or its university _____

6. Releasing _____

7. Carnival attraction with rifles and targets _____

8. Person who directs traffic near schools _____

9. Where a horse race begins _____

10. Nitrous oxide _____

11. 1992 Stephen Rea gender-bender film, with "The" _____

12. Song title preceding the lyric "How sweet the sound that saved a wretch like me" _____

13. Mirror _____

14. Joke that's repeated again and again during a show _____

15. Plane parts activated when nearing an airport _____

16. Evidence that proves someone's guilt beyond a doubt _____

Rating   Good: 9   Excellent: 13   Ace: 16

191. AYE! AYE!

In this puzzle you're given clues for two words. Add the letter I twice to the first word to get the second word.

Ex. Ecclesiastical robe / Criminal's excuse

_____ alb _____ _____ alibi _____

1. Period or point / Numbskull

_____ _____

2. Boy / Trojan War story

_____ _____

3. Acorn or cashew / Eskimo

_____ _____

4. Alternative to a CD / Capital of Taiwan

_____ _____

5. After-bath powder / Like some type

_____ _____

6. Challenges / Books secured with locks

_____ _____

7. Protesters' shout / Dry, red table wine

_____ _____

8. Actor James of "Gunsmoke" / Quality of clouds or fluff

_____ _____

9. Whose "Inferno"? / Delicious tidbits, or small, exquisite items

_____ _____

10. To get worse, as a sore / More spirited, or more argumentative

_____ _____

Rating   Good: 5   Excellent: 8   Ace: 10

192. CITY AND STATE

The first and last names of the artist EDGAR DEGAS share all but one letter—the R in EDGAR and the S in DEGAS. The name of what well-known American city shares all but one letter of the name of its state? Hint: The city has around 200,000 people, and it is one of the largest cities of its state.

193. TWISTED MEANINGS

In each pair of five-letter words here, rearrange the letters of one of them to get a synonym of the other. Which word in the pair is the anagram and which is the synonym is for you to figure out.

Ex. WIDER, EERIE __WEIRD__
[an anagram of WIDER and a synonym of "eerie"]

1. START, BINGE _____

2. TIGHT, PEACH _____

3. VALUE, THROW _____

4. REPOT, DRUNK _____

5. ROOST, TRUNK _____

6. CHASE, HURTS _____

7. EXPEL, CIVET _____

8. GREEN, CLASS _____

9. HEART, WORLD _____

10. MODEL, AILED _____

11. NEVER, CHEEK _____

12. MONEY, CRUEL _____

13. HARMS, SWAMP _____

14. GREAT, PURSE _____

Rating   Good: 9   Excellent: 12   Ace: 14

194. "CROSS" WORDS

There are two letters of the alphabet that form crosses—T and X. Every answer in this puzzle is a familiar word, name, or phrase that begins with T and ends with X.

Ex. Obsolescent, long-distance communication __Telex__

1. Government levy _____

2. Number of letters in the English alphabet _____

3. Part of the body between the neck and the abdomen _____

4. Movie cowboy with a Wonder Horse _____

5. Movie theater with three screens _____

6. Hiker's snack of nuts, raisins, dried fruit, etc. _____

7. Formal attire, informally _____

8. Large, carnivorous dinosaur _____

9. Cereal that's "for kids" _____

10. Certain spicy cuisine _____

11. Item that holds fishhooks, reels, bait, etc. _____

12. Watch that "takes a licking and keeps on ticking" _____

13. Brand-name product that gives cars a shine _____

14. Musical instrument played by Bill Clinton _____

15. Strike motionless with amazement or terror _____

16. Feature of many fancy dictionaries and thesauruses _____

Rating   Good: 9   Excellent: 13   Ace: 16

195. ONE AND THE SAME

For each word below, provide a synonym in which the first two letters are the same as the last two letters of the word provided.

Ex. Combat __attack__

1. Educate _____

2. Church _____

3. Umpire _____

4. Choose _____

5. Collar _____

6. Blunder _____

7. Arctic _____

8. Madden _____

9. Swerve _____

10. Push _____

11. Bush _____

12. Stupid _____

13. Brain _____

14. Antennae _____

In the following examples, the last three letters of the given word are the first three letters of the synonym:

15. Ample _____

16. Eating _____

17. Total _____

18. Flabbergast _____

Rating   Good: 13   Excellent: 16   Ace: 18

196. SOUND OF THE CITY

Boston and Austin are two well-known American cities whose six-letter names rhyme. What two well-known American cities have nine-letter names that rhyme?

197. EXTRA EFFORT

Every answer in this puzzle is a familiar two-word phrase in which both words start with E.

Ex. Sharp perception, like a bird's ___*eagle eye*___

1. Something that's dyed each spring _____

2. Shocking fish _____

3. Way to leave in case of a fire _____

4. Area formerly behind the Iron Curtain _____

5. What Reagan once called the Soviet Union _____

6. Minimal use of power, as in modern appliances _____

7. Where to get a visa to see the Great Pyramids _____

8. The S.A.T., for example _____

9. How Madrileños speak _____

10. Houseplants whose leaves resemble parts of a pachyderm

_____

11. P.M. issue of a newspaper _____

12. Teaching of grades K-6 _____

13. Charles Lamb or Alexander Pope _____

14. An expert in the field of machine wiring and supplying power

_____

15. Old-style newsboy's cry _____

Rating   Good: 9   Excellent: 12   Ace: 15

198. SMOOTH MOVE

In each of the following words, take one letter and move it to a new position to get a new word.

Ex. HOTELS ___HOSTEL___ [moving the S to between the O and T]

1. ABOARD _____

2. AUCTION _____

3. TICKLER _____

4. GALLERY _____

5. GUIANA _____

6. HEARTEN _____

7. ACCUSER _____

8. IMMERSED _____

9. WHITER _____

10. UNIONS _____

11. BEING [two answers] _____ _____

12. LARGE [two answers] _____ _____

Rating Good: 8 Excellent: 11 Ace: 14 (including both parts of #11 and #12)

199. "IF I WERE U ..."

Each sentence below has two blanks. The word that goes in the first blank has an I as its initial vowel. Change that I to a U and you'll get a new word that goes in the second blank to complete the sentence.

Ex. At the golf course, the expert had to ___*differ*___ with the ___*duffer*___ on the best way to play the hole.

1. Newsbreak: Exercise guru Richard _____ just received a traffic _____ for speeding.

2. For the new Tarzan movie the ad writer composed a funny _____ about life in the _____.

3. It was under the hammer and _____ that the committed Communist mother would _____ her baby.

4. To some young moviegoers, "Play _____ for Me" is just a _____ old film.

5. The slightly chunky singer wants to _____ before she does a _____ with her svelte cousin.

6. I'm so sensitive about proper procedure that when the card dealer started to _____ the cards incorrectly, it would _____ my feathers.

7. If a serious statesman acts uncharacteristically _____ on national TV, it may _____ his good reputation.

8. When the thief tried to pull a _____ on the _____ [hyph. wd.] old woman, she thought he was going to give *her* money!

Rating Good: 4 Excellent: 6 Ace: 8

200. PURE FICTION

Rearrange the 10 letters in the word SUPEROXIDE to name a famous fictional character. Who is it?

ANSWERS

1. THE SWITCH IS ON
1. Naughty, nice
2. Fast, slow
3. Pass, fail
4. Tender, tough
5. Bright, dumb
6. Rookie, expert
7. Aid, hinder
8. Short, tall
9. Great, small
10. Brave, scared
11. Host, guest
12. Sober, loaded

2. I C CLEARLY NOW
1. Ice cream
2. Internal combustion
3. Irish coffee
4. Iron Curtain
5. Ivory Coast
6. Indian corn
7. Insurance company
8. Immaculate Conception
9. Inferiority complex
10. Intensive care
11. Inspector Clouseau
12. Imogene Coca
13. Integral calculus
14. "I, Claudius"
15. Instant camera
16. Index card
17. Interstate commerce
18. Inaugural committee

3. LOOKING UP
1. United Press
2. Upright piano
3. Union Pacific
4. Upper Peninsula
5. Under par
6. Units place
7. Unusual punishment
8. University press
9. Utility pole
10. Umbrella policy (or plan)
11. Universal pictures

12. Underarm perspiration
13. Uranium plant
14. Ukulele player
15. Unsalted peanuts

4. SCRAMBLED OPPOSITES
In, passé

5. URBAN SOUNDS
1. Phoenix
2. Lansing
3. Cheyenne
4. Boulder
5. Juneau
6. Dover
7. Boise
8. Casper
9. Dallas
10. Fargo
11. Macon
12. Wheeling
13. Billings
14. Reading or Redding
15. Skokie
16. Yuma
17. Gary
18. Reno
19. York
20. Hilo

6. SHADES OF SEPTEMBER
1. License plate
2. Goose pimples
3. Surprise party
4. Rose petal
5. Noise pollution
6. Grease pencil
7. Pease porridge
8. Cheese puffs (or cheese pops)
9. Mouse pad
10. Primrose path
11. Blaise Pascal
12. "Melrose Place"
13. Lacrosse player
14. Reverse psychology

7. UP TO NO GOOD

1. Eggnog
2. Nonagon
3. Ingénue
4. Aging
5. Noggin
6. Engaging
7. Gauguin
8. Ginning
9. Nagano
10. Gonging
11. Genuine
12. Going on
13. Gaining on
14. Nag, nag, nag
15. Going, going, gone

8. STRING QUINTET

Commonplace

9. DO IT WITH ZEAL

1. Zilch
2. Lopez
3. Blazer
4. Lizard
5. Sleazy
6. Brazil
7. Lorenz
8. Nozzle
9. Schulz
10. Valdez
11. Denzel
12. Seltzer
13. Gazelle
14. Waltzes
15. Dazzler
16. Berlitz
17. Sizable
18. Pretzel

10. MOVE TO THE REAR

1. Alloy, loyal
2. Never, Verne
3. Intra, train
4. Angle, glean
5. Libel, Belli
6. Roast, Astro
7. Manor, "Norma"
8. Amass, Assam
9. Aside, ideas

10. Señor, Norse
11. Petri, tripe
12. State, A-test

11. "8" LINKS

1. State
2. Weight
3. Plate
4. Straight
5. Date
6. Great
7. Rate
8. Slate
9. Late
10. Mate
11. Freight
12. Gate

12. HEAD CASE

Searching (ear, chin)

13. TAKING YOUR CUES

1. Cucumber
2. Cupid
3. Cubism
4. Cumulus
5. Cuneiform
6. Cupola
7. Cutaneous
8. Kew Gardens
9. Cue card
10. Cusack
11. Cunard
12. Cubicle
13. Cue ball
14. Cumulative
15. Kyushu
16. Cuticle
17. Kewpie
18. Cutie (or cutie pie)

14. SHHH!

1. Jeep, sheep
2. Jelly, Shelley
3. Jingle, shingle
4. Jail, shale
5. Joan, shown
6. Jaded, shaded
7. Jerk, shirk
8. Jutting, shutting

9. Jimmy, shimmy
10. Jekyll, shekel
11. Joey, showy
12. Jackals, shackles

15. S & L
1. Lasso
2. Seles
3. Ellis
4. Lisle
5. Lassie
6. Assail
7. Lessee
8. Leslie
9. Soleil
10. La Salle
11. Useless
12. Silesia
13. Selassie
14. I'll see
15. As usual
16. All Souls'

16. AUTHOR! AUTHOR!
(William Dean) Howells, H.G. Wells

17. ANALOGIES
1. Deer (male of the animal spelled backward)
2. Overcome (opposite of each half of the word)
3. Haha (second and fourth letters the same, and the next letter of the alphabet of the first and third letters)
4. Nonagon or enneagon (geometrical figure with the number of sides indicated by the number at the end of the word)
5. Riding (first three letters moved to the end)
6. Mississippi (state name formed by repeating the letters of the word as many times as necessary)
7. Croquet or polo (game played with the equipment named by changing the second letter of the word from U to A)
8. Continue … or any synonym of this word (meaning of the word when considered as a phrase, with a space in the middle [be at, go on])

9. Tubs (each letter in the word shifted one space later in the alphabet)
10. Lynx (animal whose name completes a punning phrase [chocolate mousse, missing links])
11. Philippines (country whose capital is an anagram of the previous word [Athens, Manila])

18. CONNECTING A TO B
1. Lima bean
2. Prima ballerina
3. Sofa bed
4. Ouija board
5. Opera buff
6. Panda bear
7. Aurora Borealis
8. Data base (or data bank)
9. Plea bargain
10. Camera bag
11. Santa Barbara
12. Tampa Bay
13. Fiesta Bowl
14. Atlanta Braves
15. Flea bite
16. Polka band
17. Encyclopaedia Britannica
18. Daytona Beach
19. Sea breeze
20. Pajama bottom(s)

19. ION DISPLAY
1. Stall, stallion
2. Convent, convention
3. Miss, mission
4. Bill, billion
5. Divers, diversion
6. Accord, accordion
7. Compass, compassion
8. Avers, aversion
9. Benedict, benediction

20. NICKNAMES
Ricochet

21. SPINNING LP'S
1. Pupil
2. Apollo
3. Appall
4. Appeal

5. Pileup
6. People
7. Paella
8. Lollipop
9. Pull-up
10. Pep pill
11. Pale ale
12. Plop plop
13. Pope Paul
14. Apple pie
15. Lap pool
16. Lippo Lippi

22. WHOSE WHAT?
1. Hearst's ears
2. Starr's tar
3. Brooks's rook
4. Brando's rand
5. Astaire's stair
6. O'Toole's tool
7. Masters's aster
8. Trump's rum
9. Glover's love
10. Styron's tyro
11. Spinks's pink
12. Prowse's rows
13. Spencer's pence
14. Granger's range
15. Dalton's alto
16. Crockett's rocket
17. Bridges's ridge
18. Chandler's handle

23. MOTHER'S DAY
1. Amherst
2. Destroy
3. Earshot
4. Hamster
5. Maestro
6. Roasted
7. Samoyed
8. Hydrate
9. Threads
10. Dahomey
11. Modesty
12. Someday
13. Thermos
14. Stardom
15. Hardest

24. P.U.
Shy (pushy)

25. RADIO DIAL
1. Fan mail
2. Filet mignon
3. Flea market
4. Flour mill
5. Folding money
6. Free market
7. Face mask
8. Flying machine
9. Folk music
10. Fort McHenry
11. Fu Manchu
12. First Monday
13. Fannie Mae
14. Family medicine
15. Fire marshal
16. Foot massage
17. Foreign minister
18. Full monty

26. 4 X 4
1. Game show
2. Look into
3. Slip away or slog away
4. Fast lane or fair lady
5. Root beer
6. Ship ahoy
7. Book shop or body shop or boat show
8. Life span
9. Love nest or Loch Ness
10. Lamb stew

Note: Other answers may also be possible.

27. RH FACTOR
1. Red herring
2. Rest home (or retirement home)
3. Right hand
4. Road hog
5. Robin Hood
6. Rocking horse
7. Rubber hose
8. Rosh Hashanah
9. Royal Highness
10. Rocky Horror
11. Relative humidity
12. Round hole

13. Rush hour
14. Record holder
15. Riverdale High
16. Random House

28. PROFESSIONAL MIX-UP
Astrophysicist, psychiatrists

29. FILM ADAPTATION
1. "The Silence of the Lambs"
2. "From Here to Eternity"
3. "In the Heat of the Night"
4. "American Beauty"
5. "Dances with Wolves"
6. "Rain Man"
7. "The Sound of Music"
8. "Annie Hall"
9. "Rocky"
10. "Hamlet"
11. "Marty"
12. "Amadeus"
13. "Platoon"
14. "Ordinary People"
15. "Lawrence of Arabia"
16. "The Godfather"
17. "Braveheart"
18. "On the Waterfront"

30. TRIPLE RHYME
1. Blackjack plaque
2. Downtown gown
3. Sneak peek week
4. Shock jock clock
5. Cookbook crook
6. Snail mail scale
7. Space race base (or place)
8. Plain Jane swain
9. Shareware fair
10. Hong Kong song
11. Dream Team scheme
12. Chop shop swap
13. Night light height
14. Backpack snack

31. SOMETHING I OWE
1. Silo
2. Rhino
3. Gyro
4. Fido

5. Nitro
6. Shiloh
7. "Psycho"
8. Tyro
9. Geico
10. Sligo
11. Hydro
12. Pyro
13. Cairo
14. Hypo
15. Wino
16. Dido
17. Tae-Bo
18. High-low
19. Pie dough
20. Heigh-ho

32. GEOGRAPHICAL PARTS
Thailand (tail, hand)

33. L.A. DREAMING
1. Dalai Lama
2. Lake Placid
3. Alan Ladd
4. Burglar alarm
5. Solar flare
6. Planck's Law
7. La Scala
8. Malay Peninsula
9. Petula Clark
10. Latin class
11. Lawn display
12. Falkland Islands
13. Lacrosse player
14. Slave labor
15. Black Plague
16. Last place

34. OPPOSITE ENDS
1. Last
2. Far
3. Ill
4. Under
5. Minor
6. Death
7. Arrive
8. Sundown
9. Guest
10. Loose

11. Liquid
12. Assure
13. Separate
14. Fire
15. Reject
16. Receive
17. Tarry
18. Conceal
19. Adept
20. Father

35. R.N.'S
1. Real name
2. Roman numeral
3. Royal Navy
4. Right now
5. Republican nomination
6. Ralph Nader
7. Robin's nest
8. Round number
9. Romance novel
10. Runny nose
11. Radio network
12. Ricky Nelson
13. Richard Nixon
14. Rusty nail
15. Ransom note

36. DISPLAYING LEADERSHIP
Indira Gandhi

37. A LITTLE T.L.C.
1. Plate
2. Bell
3. Light
4. Test
5. Union
6. Box
7. Suit
8. Top
9. Service
10. Neck

38. SERVING OF P'S
1. Thumb, thump
2. Gallon, gallop
3. Wallow, wallop
4. Sheer, sheep
5. Swami, swamp

6. Overlay, overlap
7. Hedgehog, hedgehop
8. Share, shark, sharp

39. ON YOUR TOES
1. October
2. Halitosis
3. Toady
4. Saratoga
5. Togo
6. Tojo
7. Token
8. Anatoly
9. Potomac
10. Total
11. Totem
12. Krakatoa
13. Manitoba
14. Tobit
15. Daytona
16. Rigatoni

40. A CAPITAL IDEA
Khartoum, cartoon

41. SO TH-TH-THERE!
1. Well, wealth
2. Tea, teeth
3. Bow, both
4. Slew, sleuth
5. Four, forth
6. Myrrh, mirth
7. Hell, health
8. Sics, sixth
9. Bred, breadth
10. Sow, south

42. THE LIVING END
1. Seven days
2. Open door
3. Batten down
4. Frozen daiquiri
5. Golden Delicious
6. Sudden death
7. Stephen Douglas
8. Chicken dog
9. Mogen David
10. Queen dowager
11. Ten Downing

12. Kitchen drawer
13. Allen Drury
14. Ellen DeGeneres
15. Halloween decorations
16. Häagen-Dazs

14. Ipanema
15. Aeneas
16. Needle
17. Incognito
18. Ebenezer

43. ALLITERATIVE FOURS
1. "West Wing"
2. Test tube
3. Stop sign
4. Work week
5. Love life
6. Road rage
7. Lady Luck
8. Dead duck
9. Live long
10. Soap suds
11. Soft spot
12. Full fare

44. SWEARING-IN
Orangutan (nine letters)

45. "U.S." GEOGRAPHY
1. Columbus
2. Augusta
3. Syracuse
4. Houston
5. Tuscaloosa
6. Sandusky
7. Muskogee
8. Massachusetts
9. Susquehanna
10. Rushmore

46. KNEE-HIGH
1. Geneva
2. Nina
3. Toscanini
4. Nemo
5. Anemic
6. Nikkei
7. Neeson
8. Benito
9. Neither
10. Polynesian
11. Nissan
12. Neon
13. Nero

47. CPR EXAM
1. Wave
2. Ball
3. Light
4. Board
5. Card
6. House
7. Room
8. Table
9. Guard
10. Gun

48. ON A FIRST-NAME BASIS
Casey, Elsie

49. BLANKETY-BLANK
1. Bride & groom
2. Horse & buggy
3. Large & small
4. Flesh & blood
5. Short & sweet
6. Track & field
7. Bread & water
8. Death & taxes
9. Power & light
10. Peace & quiet
11. Right & wrong
12. Rough & ready
13. Twist & shout
14. Point & click

50. TRIPLE THREAT
1. Muumuu mover
2. Sing Sing singer
3. Yo-yo yodel
4. Cuckoo coupon
5. Dodo domain (or domicile)
6. Cancan candidate
7. Bonbon bonfire
8. Chowchow chowder
9. Chi-chi Sheila
10. Boo-boo boutonniere
11. Rah-rah Roger

12. No-no notion
13. Choo-choo chooser
14. Walla Walla wallaby

51. A "NEW" PUZZLE
1. One way
2. Stone wall
3. Rhine wine or fine wine
4. Paine Webber
5. Lone wolf
6. Joanne Woodward
7. Machine-wash
8. Maxine Waters
9. Medicine woman
10. Feminine wiles
11. Engine wear
12. Mine workers
13. Telephone wire
14. Done with

52. DOUBLE OCCUPANCY
Automobile insurance

53. TOUCHDOWN!
1. Tap dance (or dancing)
2. Test drive
3. Tone deafness
4. Tooth decay
5. Telephone directory
6. Ten Days
7. Tax deduction
8. "Taxi Driver"
9. Technical difficulties
10. T'ang dynasty
11. Top dog
12. Tongue depressor
13. "Tin Drum"
14. Tasmanian devil
15. Teapot Dome
16. Turkey Day

54. LAND SAKES!
1. Russia (rush ya)
2. Ukraine (you crane)
3. Sudan (sue Dan)
4. Samoa (some more)
5. Kenya (can ya)
6. Norway (nor weigh)
7. Denmark (then Mark)

8. Japan (d'ja pan)
9. Pakistan (pack is tan)

55. SAY WHAT?
1. Saber
2. Sacred
3. Salem
4. Savor
5. Sajak
6. Cézanne
7. Safer
8. Sable
9. Seiko
10. Sadism
11. Sega
12. Sailor
13. Saline
14. Satyr
15. Seychelles
16. Seder
17. Sagan
18. Sapiens

56. CHANGE OF LEADERS
Bine, cine, dine, fine, kine, line, mine, nine, pine, sine, tine, vine, wine, zine

57. ANA-DECLARATIONS
1. Limbaugh
2. Marciano
3. Feinstein
4. Dangerfield
5. Eisenhower
6. Gainsborough
7. Chamberlain
8. Polanski
9. DiCaprio
10. Hammerstein
11. Lichtenstein
12. Hemingway
13. Westinghouse
14. Kristofferson

58. GOING OUT ON A LIMB
1. Bubble gum
2. Whole grain
3. Battle ground
4. Jungle gym
5. Durable goods

6. Yale graduate
7. Staple gun
8. Estelle Getty
9. Miracle Gro
10. Tattletale gray
11. Table game
12. Flammable gas
13. Missile gap
14. Idle gossip
15. Gobble gobble

59. LONG JUMP
1. Lake, leak, like
2. Slate, sleet, slight
3. Nail, kneel, Nile
4. Crepes, creeps, cripes
5. Stale, steal, style
6. Sane, seen, sign
7. Waves, weaves, wives
8. Spade, speed, spied
9. Later, liter, lighter

60. NAME SQUARE
The following are three possible answers.
Your square may be different.

TODD	TONY	LEON
OMAR	OLAV	ELMO
DAVE	NATE	OMAR
DREW	YVES	NORM

61. WHO KNEW?
1. Canoe
2. Ingénue
3. Keanu
4. Retinue
5. Agnew
6. Sununu
7. U Nu
8. Revenue
9. Entre nous
10. What's new?
11. Bienvenue
12. Parvenu
13. Vishnu
14. Tippecanoe
15. Renew

62. THE "F" WORD
1. First
2. Fair
3. Fame
4. Fact
5. Fine
6. Field
7. Fast
8. Fish
9. Fire
10. Far
11. Fun
12. Flesh
13. Front
14. Forgive
15. Fox
16. Food
17. Fits
18. Fore
19. Forever
20. Few

63. COLORFUL LANGUAGE
1. Slip
2. Heart
3. Tide
4. Pages
5. Monday
6. Cedar
7. Sale
8. Sugar
9. List
10. Screen
11. Wolf
12. Petals
13. Record
14. Berets

64. CHANGE OF APPAREL
Dressing down, dressing gown

65. SAN FRANCISCO
1. Fast
2. Fresh
3. Freedom
4. Frown
5. Fat
6. Fail
7. Fall
8. Foolish, fat-headed
9. Faint, feeble, frail, fragile
10. Forerunner

11. Fertile, filthy
12. Flexible, floppy, flaccid
13. Freshman, first-year
14. Fraternity
15. Frequent(ly)

66. R. & D.
1. Reader
2. Rudder
3. Derriere
4. Adder
5. Reorder
6. Raider
7. Dürer
8. Radar
9. Radioed
10. Derided
11. Do-or-die
12. Air raid
13. Red deer
14. Dead air
15. Rear door
16. Dear diary

67. LOOSE ENDS
1. Praising, raisin
2. Foregone, Oregon
3. Crockery, rocker
4. Overdone, Verdon
5. Turbaned, urbane
6. Foodless, oodles
7. Flattest, lattes
8. Tree fern, reefer
9. Fragment, ragmen
10. Traverse, ravers
11. Stampede, tamped
12. Stickler, tickle

68. THE WRITE STUFF
(Henry David) Thoreau

69. QU- QUIZ
1. Quill, kill
2. Queen, keen
3. Quite, kite
4. Quick, kick
5. Quartz, courts
6. Quote, coat
7. Qualms, calms
8. Quirk, Kirk
9. Quaver, caver
10. Quilter, kilter

70. FOR DEAR OLD DAD
1. Lace, palace
2. Tricks, Patrick's
3. Nicked, panicked
4. Rental, parental
5. Ella, paella
6. Tina, patina
7. Tent, patent
8. Trolled, patrolled
9. Inter, painter
10. Rag on, paragon

71. EXPERIENCING THE DT'S
1. Dieted
2. Idiot
3. Etude
4. Outdid
5. Dated
6. Audited
7. Ditto
8. Tut-tutted
9. To date
10. Dot-to-dot
11. Ad-out
12. Added to
13. Died out
14. Due date
15. I did it!

72. DIALING 6-8-7
Murmurous

73. PLAYING LP'S
1. License plate
2. Lily pad
3. Lake Placid
4. Law professor
5. Labour Party
6. Low point
7. Life preserver
8. Lesson plan
9. Lincoln penny
10. Lord's Prayer
11. Launch pad
12. Liquid Paper
13. "Little Prince"
14. Love potion

15. Laser printer
16. Labor pains
17. Lapel pin
18. Last place

74. NOTHING LOST
1. Orange, range
2. Opinion, pinion
3. Ozone, zone
4. Orally, rally
5. Ovary, vary
6. Oscars, scars
7. Owing, wing
8. Op art, part
9. Omission, mission
10. Oasis, as is

75. RHYME AND REASON
1. Trike or bike
2. Buzz
3. Truce
4. Stunk
5. Boat
6. Horn
7. Ritz
8. Bright
9. Ledge
10. Baker
11. Trample
12. Clock
13. Lie
14. Sheep
15. Cent
16. Hate
17. Poles
18. Troupe
19. Blue
20. Spout
21. Blot or dot
22. Thrice
23. Pyre
24. Snipe
25. Square
26. Knell

76. C-T PLANNING
Cut, connect

77. FOR MOTHER
1. This, Mathis
2. Shed, mashed
3. Trix, matrix
4. Lice, malice
5. Scot, mascot
6. Stiff, mastiff
7. Sonic, Masonic
8. Linger, malinger
9. Inland, mainland
10. Neater, man-eater

78. STARTER SWITCH
1. Ballot
2. Acid
3. Race
4. Image
5. Suspects
6. Service
7. Office
8. Accident
9. Inning
10. Poppy
11. Away
12. Anthem
13. Impossible
14. Artict
15. Number

79. AUTO ANALYSIS
1. Axle
2. Lock
3. Radio
4. Pedal
5. Wiper
6. Brake
7. Choke
8. Piston
9. Gasket
10. Fender
11. Clutch
12. Sunroof
13. Brights
14. Dashboard
15. Roll bar
16. Back seat
17. First gear
18. Spare tire

80. F AND E
Fame and fortune

81. KEEPING YOU ON YOUR TOES
1. Toga
2. Togo
3. Tojo
4. Tokyo
5. Tony
6. Totem
7. Total
8. Topiary
9. (Marisa) Tomei
10. Topaz
11. Tokens
12. Tobit
13. Torah
14. Topol
15. Toper
16. Ptomaine

82. WHAT'S IN A NAME?
1. (Ralph) Nader
2. (Gloria) Steinem
3. (Gerhardus) Mercator
4. (David) Souter
5. (Arthur) Ashe
6. (Christian) Dior
7. (Bob) Costas
8. (Fred or Adele) Astaire
9. (Ann) Landers
10. (Lily) Pons
11. (Robert E.) Lee
12. (Ira) Levin or (Irving) Stone

83. IN FRONT
1. Tuition, intuition
2. Carnation, incarnation
3. Spire, inspire
4. Dentures, indentures
5. Fringe, infringe
6. Sense, incense
7. Fur, infer
8. Curd, incurred
9. Jest, ingest
10. Great, ingrate
11. Sighed, inside
12. Clued, include

84. ROMAN NUMERALS
Climaxed (8 letters, including all but V).
The word "exclaimed" (9 letters) also uses all
but V. The phrase "voice mailbox" (12 letters)
uses all but D.

85. PACKING ON THE POUNDS
1. Little lamb
2. Left jab
3. Lunch club
4. Light bulb
5. Lynch mob
6. Linking verb
7. Lenin's Tomb
8. Language lab
9. Lobster bib
10. Lion cub
11. Livery cab
12. Letter bomb
13. Lee J. Cobb
14. Life and limb

86. TWO TIMES THREE
1. Seesaw
2. Tiptoe
3. Pigpen
4. Bedbug
5. Top Ten
6. Pen pal
7. Bat boy
8. Lie low
9. "Mad Max"
10. Big Ben
11. Not now
12. Rob Roy
13. Potpie
14. For fun
15. Sunset

87. OVERLAPS
1. Fair, airy, fairy
2. Yeas, East, yeast
3. Chic, hick, chick
4. Lear, earn, learn
5. Part, arty, party
6. Bras, rash, brash
7. Tall, ally, tally
8. Wind, Indy, windy

9. Even, vent, event
10. Pain, ain't, paint

88. BEAR SESSION
Panda, Q and A

89. ALL ABOUT ME
1. Mount Everest
2. Middle East
3. Mister Ed
4. Medical examiner
5. Managing editor
6. Mechanical engineer
7. Montreal Expo
8. Mesozoic Era
9. Manila envelope
10. Main event
11. Mixed emotions
12. "Midnight Express"
13. Modern English
14. "My eye!"
15. Mental exercise

90. DOUBLE F'S
1. Sniff
2. Gaffe
3. Afford
4. Baffle
5. Tariff
6. Buffet
7. Effort
8. Ruffle
9. Affair
10. Stiffen
11. Muffler
12. Pontiff
13. Scuffle
14. Sheriff
15. Souffle
16. Affluent
17. Suffrage
18. Tradeoff

91. UPS AND DOWNS
1. Touch up, touchdown
2. Roundup, round down
3. Show up, showdown
4. Crack up, crackdown
5. Holdup, hold down
6. Stand-up, stand down
7. Shakeup, shakedown
8. Dress up, dress down
9. Breakup, breakdown
10. Sit-up, sit-down
11. Cutup, cut down
12. Shut up, shutdown

92. FIRST FIVE
Debacle

93. TWO G'S
1. Guinea pig
2. Goose egg
3. Global warming
4. Gas rationing
5. Greek flag
6. Glass blowing
7. Gift wrapping
8. Grab bag
9. Grade crossing
10. Get along (git along)
11. "Gold Bug"
12. G string
13. Guide dog
14. Gone fishing

94. TRADING PLACES
1. Goal, gaol
2. Hola, halo
3. Organ, argon
4. Bossa, basso
5. Conan, canon
6. Tonga, tango
7. Coral, carol
8. Op art, aport
9. Co-star, castor
10. Octane, act one

95. IT'S COLD!
1. Burgundy
2. Berlin
3. Burlesque
4. Burlap
5. Burnett
6. Birmingham
7. Burlington
8. Bermuda
9. Burgeon

10. Burma
11. Burkina Faso
12. Burglar
13. Berserk
14. Burger
15. Burgoyne
16. Bursitis
17. "Bernadette"
18. Burbank

96. WORD'S WORTH
Peyote
Other answers: layette and Tetley (brand name)

97. ANIMAL PENS
1. Horse
2. Monkey
3. Cat
4. Dog
5. Tiger
6. Hog
7. Rat
8. Elephant
9. Fox
10. Lion
11. Wolf
12. Mouse
13. Sheep
14. Bear

98. A PUZZLE? OY!
1. Later, loiter
2. Haste, hoist
3. Painter, pointer
4. Braille, broil
5. Maced, moist
6. Daily, doily
7. Pays, poise
8. Frayed, Freud
9. Baylor, boiler
10. Chase, choice

99. M & M'S
1. Drum major
2. Skim milk
3. Swim meet
4. "Phantom Menace"
5. Freedom march

6. Jim Morrison
7. Tom Mix
8. Sam Malone
9. From Mars
10. Quantum mechanics
11. Sodium monoxide
12. Farm machinery (or machines)
13. Team mascot
14. Thom McAn
15. William McKinley

100. EVEN OUT
Buoyant, boat

101. "V" FOR VICTORY
1. Veer
2. Vain
3. Viral
4. Viand
5. Vacate
6. Volley
7. Virgin
8. Vetoed
9. Vector
10. Valiant
11. Verbose
12. Vaguest
13. Violated
14. Versatile
15. Vice-presidents

102. LEADING SAINTS
1. Sand trap
2. "Star Trek"
3. Swim trunks
4. Sales tax
5. Spare tire
6. Sea turtle or sea tortoise
7. Siamese twins
8. Soft touch
9. Slide trombone
10. Sweet tooth
11. Spring training
12. Soccer team
13. Substitute teacher
14. Steak tartare
15. State tree

103. T-SER

1. Treasure
2. Temper
3. Table
4. Touch
5. Tongue
6. Terrible
7. Train or tenure
8. Telephone or toe
9. Test, toothpaste, or television
10. Tow, tandem, or tank
11. Top
12. Tourist
13. Time
14. Turkey

104. THAT'S ENTERTAINMENT

Ben Stiller, Glenn Miller

105. BOSTON TALK

1. Tampa, tamper
2. Lima, lemur
3. Inca, inker
4. Manna, manner
5. Monica, moniker
6. Papa, popper
7. Tuna, tuner
8. Conga, conger
9. Panda, pander
10. Cornea, cornier

106. TWO TO THREE

1. Diploma
2. Baloney
3. Informant
4. Apostle
5. Forgotten
6. Quadruple
7. Determine
8. Survival or salival
9. Papyrus
10. Epistle
11. Bonanza
12. Collegian
13. Lieutenant
14. Intrepid
15. Clairvoyance
16. Curmudgeon

107. ALL LIES

1. Lysol (made by L & F Consumer Products)
2. Libel (written defamation)
3. Liabilities (minus side)
4. Lilac (mentioned in Whitman's elegy to Lincoln)
5. Lima (green pods)
6. Limey (British sailor)
7. Lyons (movie critic)
8. Library (librarian Melvil Dewey, not Adm. George Dewey)
9. Liberia (capital is Monrovia)
10. License (usually not gettable until age 16)
11. Lycanthropy (assumption by humans of animal form)
12. Liposuction (done to decrease one's weight)
13. Linotype (German)
14. Liza (Lerner and Loewe)

108. SHIFTY, SHIFTY

Inkier, purply

109. HOMOPHONE PAIRS

1. Wore, piece (war and peace)
2. Reed, right (read and write)
3. Hyde, Sikh (hide and seek)
4. Pease, queues (P's and Q's)
5. Daze, knights (days and nights)
6. Hart, sole (heart and soul)
7. Whine, dyne (wine and dine)
8. Won, awl (one and all)
9. Pic, chews (pick and choose)
10. Prose, khans (pros and cons)
11. Thyme, tied (time and tide)
12. Bye, cell (buy and sell)

110. PERSONALITY CHANGES

1. Patsy Cline
2. Ricky Martin
3. Rob Lowe
4. Sean Connery
5. Bruce Jenner
6. Chuck Norris
7. Pierre Cardin
8. Ray Milland
9. Ross Perot

10. Sonny Bono
11. Willie Mays
12. Bert Parks
13. Boris Becker
14. Clara Barton
15. Zero Mostel

111. E FOR EFFORT
1. Egg white
2. Easter parade
3. Entry fee
4. Elbow grease
5. Emerald Isle
6. Empire State
7. Exhaust pipe
8. Exchange rate
9. Eau Claire
10. Emergency brake
11. En garde
12. Escape clause
13. Eskimo Pie
14. Executive privilege
15. Evergreen tree
16. End zone

112. ALL BUT Q
Chintzy, fjords, gawk, plumb, vex

113. UNITED NATIONS
1. France
2. Brazil
3. Greece
4. Indonesia
5. Jamaica
6. Slovenia
7. Maldives
8. Lebanon
9. Algeria
10. Costa Rica
11. Uganda
12. Cape Verde

114. LETTER ROTATION
1. Boone, booze
2. Nero, zero
3. Crane, craze
4. Bono, bozo
5. Seine, seize
6. Nipper, zipper
7. Maine, maize
8. Funny, fuzzy

115. DEEJAYS
1. Dust jacket
2. Double Jeopardy
3. Dow Jones
4. Diamond jubilee
5. Dear John
6. Daily journal
7. Dr. Jekyll
8. Def Jam
9. Dixieland jazz
10. Denim jeans
11. Dirty joke
12. Dumb jock
13. Door jamb
14. Day job
15. Don Juan

116. HOMOPHONIC GEOGRAPHY
Iran and Niger (rain and reign)

117. PAIR-A-GRAMS
1. Song & dance
2. Fast & loose
3. Live & learn
4. Pure & simple
5. Part & parcel
6. North & south
7. Large & small
8. Aches & pains
9. Sugar & spice
10. Older & wiser
11. Right & wrong
12. Hale & hearty
13. Past & present
14. Stars & stripes
15. Search & rescue

118. LISPED INITIALS
1. Sore thumb
2. Second thoughts
3. Stone's throw
4. Strike three
5. Speech therapy
6. Set theory
7. Strom Thurmond
8. Summer theater

9. Spring thaw
10. Surgical thread
11. September third
12. Six thousand
13. Sneak thief
14. See things

119. TWO MORE
1. IT (bandit, pulpit)
2. CH (starch, blotch)
3. AN (seaman, tartan)
4. OW (bestow, fellow)
5. HY (dinghy, marshy)
6. TE (demote, gamete)
7. UE (statue, tongue)
8. AR (dollar, hangar)
9. CE (fleece, pierce)
10. DY (brandy, comedy)
11. HE (clothe, soothe)
12. RN (modern, untorn)
13. AT (caveat, combat)
14. ET (bullet, rocket)
15. EL (bushel, diesel)

120. DOWNTOWN
Shoe shop

121. NOTHING TO IT
1. Corner, coroner
2. String, storing
3. Roster, rooster
4. Carton, cartoon
5. Top Cat, topcoat
6. Harp on, harpoon
7. Forger, forgoer
8. Curtly, courtly
9. Batman, boatman
10. Caster, coaster
11. Lasses, lassoes
12. Cornet, coronet

122. TRIBUTE TO MISS FITZGERALD
1. "Cinderella"
2. Mozzarella
3. Panetella
4. Rubella
5. Isabella
6. Barbarella
7. Umbrella

8. Salmonella
9. A cappella
10. Patella
11. Flagella
12. Cerebella
13. Tarantella
14. Novella
15. "Stella!"

123. MANNER OF SPEAKING
1. Master of ceremonies
2. Maid of honor
3. Moment of truth
4. Mother of pearl
5. Milk of magnesia
6. Margin of error
7. Matter of principle
8. Mall of America
9. Middle of nowhere
10. "Merchant of Venice"
11. "Marriage of Figaro"
12. Mark of Zorro
13. Man of Steel
14. March of Dimes
15. Meaning of life

124. D-PLUS
Granddaddy

125. Z-E SOUND-ALIKES
1. Graze, grays
2. Freeze, frees
3. Booze, boos
4. Daze, days
5. Prize, pries
6. Breeze, Bries
7. Doze, does
8. Wheeze, whees
9. Size, sighs
10. Paralyze, pair o' lies

126. PUBLIC ADDRESS SYSTEM
1. Allow
2. Annoy
3. Ample
4. Asset
5. Axiom
6. Avert
7. Augur

8. Arrow
9. Aroma or attar
10. Armor or aegis
11. Ardor
12. Aisle or alley
13. Ashen
14. Amigo
15. Acute
16. Await
17. Adept
18. Alias

127. PREPOSITIONALLY SPEAKING
1. Skin (or sink)
2. Point
3. Times
4. Drain
5. Worse
6. Heart
7. Coast
8. Rescue
9. Time being
10. First place
11. Other hand
12. Eight ball
13. Same token
14. Drop of a hat

128. COUPLE ONLY
CU BI ST RO DE NT AL (cubist, bistro, strode, rodent, dental)

129. THE END OF THE BEGINNING
1. Wide
2. Tall
3. Going
4. Height
5. Now
6. Thin
7. Young
8. Exit
9. Enormous
10. Lead
11. Decent
12. Early
13. Nice
14. Bright, brilliant, or brainy
15. Debark, disembark, deplane, or detrain
16. Destroy

17. Harsh or hairy
18. Safe
19. Twisted, twisty, or turning
20. Together

130. EXTRA POUNDS
1. Label
2. Bauble
3. Albee
4. Bailee
5. Libel
6. Liable
7. Aboil
8. Bobble
9. Balboa
10. Ali Baba
11. LaBelle
12. Babble
13. Billable
14. Bluebell
15. Boola-boola
16. Alibi
17. Oil bill
18. "Blue Boy"
19. Lullaby
20. "Bill Bailey"
21. Baby blue
22. Bubble boy

131. R & R
1. For rent
2. Honor roll
3. Locker room
4. Diaper rash
5. Car rental
6. Cedar Rapids
7. Choir robe
8. Meter reader
9. Peter Rabbit
10. Sugar Ray
11. Voter registration
12. Mister Rogers
13. Water rationing
14. Far right
15. Poor Richard
16. Air raid

132. THE THREE B'S
Buster Crabbe

133. WHAT OF IT?
1. Comedy
2. Coat
3. Cream
4. Crack
5. Can
6. Cast
7. Creature
8. Call
9. Crime
10. Court
11. Cause
12. Country
13. Cross
14. Code (or cone)

134. ENDS FLIPPED
1. Lustful
2. Entwine
3. Newsmen
4. Surplus
5. Macadam
6. Antenna
7. Espouse
8. Cardiac
9. Thought
10. Addenda
11. Dogwood
12. Turnout

135. SHE'S BACK!
1. Balled, called, etc.
2. Mutate
3. Generic or sceneries
4. Keener
5. Harass
6. Lanolin
7. Stablemate, stableman, or disablement
8. Disengage
9. Irretrievable
10. Management
Note: Other answers may also be possible

136. TO SURVIVE … OR FAIL
Bail out

137. WHO'S THAT SINGING?
1. Presley
2. Andrews

3. Baker
4. Charles
5. Damone
6. Darin
7. Horne
8. Loggins
9. Pride
10. Sebastian
11. Shore
12. Stewart
13. Tormé
14. Rimes
15. Strait
16. Streisand

138. DOUBLE-A
1. Straight face
2. Freight train
3. Space Age or space race
4. Rain date
5. Great Dane
6. Chain mail
7. Trade name
8. Bake sale
9. Weight gain
10. Eight days
11. Bay State
12. Slave state
13. Snail's pace
14. Brain waves

139. THREE TO ONE
1. Rocker, corker
2. Dawdle, waddle
3. Sumter, muster
4. Penal, Nepal
5. Puree, rupee
6. Retrace, terrace
7. Viral, rival
8. Milestone, limestone
9. Bolster, lobster
10. Lemons, melons (either order)

140. LET'S BE REALISTIC
Faces facts

141. HOW ODD!
1. Beatnik
2. Bargain

3. Crackle
4. Collude or culture
5. Crumble
6. Furlong
7. Galleon
8. Leopard or leotard
9. Perform
10. Rhombus
11. Skillet
12. Sunlamp
13. Support
14. Theorem
15. Torture

142. READY? ACTION!
1. Bat
2. Stamp
3. Tap
4. Can
5. Lick
6. Pan
7. Mind
8. Blow
9. Pen
10. Crack
11. Draw
12. Cast

143. BY THE DOZEN
1. Months in a Year
2. Signs of the Zodiac
3. Days of Christmas
4. Apostles (of Jesus Christ)
5. Eggs in a Carton
6. Members of a Jury
7. Players on a Canadian Football Team
8. Hours on the Face of a Clock

144. SOU'WESTER
Sweet and sour

145. T FOR TWO
1. Fort, Fourth
2. True, through
3. Tankful, thankful
4. Pity, pithy
5. Tread, thread
6. Eater, ether
7. Boot, booth

8. Tie, thigh
9. Dirt, dearth
10. Hat away, Hathaway

146. THE NAME RINGS A BELL
1. Jack Paar
2. Bret Harte
3. Joan Rivers
4. Bruce Lee
5. Grace Slick
6. Kurt Weill
7. Les Paul
8. Anne Klein
9. Stan Getz
10. Yul Brynner
11. Jane Wyatt
12. Kate Moss

147. HIDDEN MYTHOLOGY
1. Hermes
2. Minerva
3. Apollo
4. Poseidon
5. Athena
6. Artemis
7. Neptune
8. Aurora
9. Uranus
10. Phoebe
11. Persephone
12. Prometheus

148. GIRL TO BOY
Diane, Duane

149. D'OH!
1. Colorado
2. Toledo
3. Tornado
4. Aficionado
5. "Mikado"
6. Avocado
7. Fido
8. Judo
9. Crescendo
10. Tuxedo
11. Bravado
12. Innuendo
13. Commando

14. Desperado
15. Torpedo
16. Eldorado
17. Libido
18. Dodo

11. Goal posts
12. Snow globe
13. Rolled oats
14. Close quotes

150. LOSING IT

1. Britain (brain)
2. Agitate (agate)
3. Whiten (when)
4. Gravity (gravy)
5. Visitor (visor)
6. Burrito (burro)
7. Aitches (aches)
8. Celerity (celery)
9. Composite (compose)
10. Subtitle (subtle)

151. FORE-AND-AFT RHYMES

1. Bird
2. Room or hall
3. Stand
4. Way
5. Well
6. Hole
7. Point
8. Ball
9. Pot
10. Master
11. Light
12. Board
13. Call
14. Handle
15. Line

152. HALF OFF

Friend, foe

153. OH! OH!

1. Nose cone
2. Rose Bowl
3. Toll road
4. Phone home
5. "Show Boat"
6. Whole note
7. Go broke
8. Old Gold
9. Chrome dome
10. No vote

154. SMALL DIFFERENCE

1. Fire (hire)
2. Peak (weak)
3. Waning (waxing)
4. Crass (class)
5. Black (blank)
6. Brawn (brain)
7. Lightly (tightly)
8. Bucking (backing)
9. Comely (homely)
10. Acidly (avidly)
11. Nine (none)
12. Failing (sailing)
13. Hell (help)
14. Wild (mild)
15. Ejected (elected)

155. POSTSCRIPT

1. Dipstick
2. Hopscotch
3. Pipsqueak
4. Ripsaw or whipsaw
5. Sapsucker
6. Topspin
7. Campsite
8. Lipstick
9. Deep-six
10. Slapstick
11. Soupspoon
12. Stepson
13. Cheapskate
14. Sheepskin
15. Sweepstakes

156. HEAD-TO-TAIL SHIFT

Eponymous (pony, mouse)

157. IF IT'S ALL THE SAME TO YOU

1. Peek, pique
2. Groan, grown
3. Rite, right
4. Prays, praise
5. Waist, waste
6. Rowed, rode

7. Liar, lyre
8. Leased, least
9. Knead, need
10. Chased, chaste
11. Assent, ascent
12. Trust, trussed

158. 150 WORDS

1. Clock (dock)
2. Clove (dove)
3. Cluck (duck)
4. Clingy (dingy)
5. Clutch (dutch)
6. Clam up (dam up)
7. Clapper (dapper)
8. Clicker (dicker)
9. Cluster (duster)
10. Clashing (dashing)
11. Clipper (dipper)
12. Cloris (Doris)

159. WHAT THE H—?

1. Tent, tenth
2. Toot, tooth
3. Bras, brash
4. Edit, Edith
5. Mars, marsh
6. Boot, booth
7. Plus, plush
8. Blanc, blanch
9. Paris, parish
10. Heart, hearth

160. REACHING THE SAME CONCLUSION
Marie Curie

161. AND WHAT?

1. Dime
2. Deal
3. Dine
4. Doom
5. Downs
6. Death
7. Dad
8. Dance
9. Dandy
10. Dear
11. Driver
12. Day
13. Dry
14. Dagger
15. Dreams
16. Dirty
17. Dashes
18. Dried
19. Determined
20. Desist
21. Destroy
22. Dragons
23. Deliver
24. Demand

162. SIMPLE AS A, B, C

1. Belt
2. Cat
3. Line
4. Car
5. Shell
6. Book
7. Board
8. Head
9. Cheese
10. Boy
11. Dog
12. Bone
13. Number
14. Suit

163. SUDDENLY SINGLE

1. Latte, late
2. Litter, liter
3. Putt, put
4. Tatters, taters
5. Matte, mate
6. Ratting, rating
7. Bitter, biter
8. Tittle, title
9. Attest, A-test

164. F TROOP
Filled, ill-fed

165. MMM …

1. Memory
2. Mumble
3. Mayhem
4. Smarmy
5. Summer
6. Mermaid
7. Milkmen

8. Rummage
9. Symptom
10. Dilemma
11. Immense
12. Mammoth
13. Mesmerism
14. Memorandum
15. Mammogram

166. JUST FOR YOU
1. Ukulele
2. Euchre
3. Yukon
4. Unique
5. Ubiquitous
6. Eucalyptus
7. Universal
8. Yucatan
9. Ulysses
10. Utopia
11. Eulogy
12. Utensil
13. Usury
14. Euclid
15. Unicorn
16. Euphoria
17. Uganda
18. Yugoslavia, Ukraine

167. HIDDEN COMPOSERS
1. Bach
2. Verdi
3. Chopin
4. Vivaldi
5. Bellini
6. Copland
7. Schumann
8. Debussy
9. Menotti
10. Elgar
11. Handel
12. Scarlatti

168. BODY LANGUAGE
Helipad (lip, head)

169. HINKITY-PINKITY
1. Quieter rioter
2. Edison's medicines
3. Thomas's promises
4. Zachary's daiquiris
5. Annual manual
6. Crueler jeweler
7. Bettering lettering
8. Mexico's Texacos
9. Pillory Hillary
10. Resident president
11. Pottery lottery
12. Medium tedium
13. History's mysteries
14. Editor's creditors
15. Barrier carrier
16. Partisan artisan
17. Rotary's coteries
18. Rubbery shrubbery

170. TWO L'S
1. Loose-leaf
2. Longlegs
3. Lovelorn
4. Landlocked
5. Lemon-lime
6. Lily-livered
7. Lackluster or lifeless
8. Landlord
9. Lowlife
10. Linkletter
11. Limelight
12. Landlubber

171. BB'S
1. Bribe
2. Rabbi
3. Abbot
4. Bebop
5. Bobcat
6. Gobble
7. Hobnob
8. Ribbon
9. Shabby
10. Absorb
11. Bramble
12. Bobsled
13. Bombast
14. Ballboy
15. Beanbag

172. BRONTE'S LETTERS
To be or not to be

173. CB TALK
1. Crystal ball
2. Cat burglar
3. Carte blanche
4. Coke bottles
5. Contract bridge
6. Coffee break
7. Cabin boy
8. Comic book
9. Cordon bleu
10. Carving board
11. Corned beef
12. Cocoa butter
13. "College Bowl"
14. Color blindness
15. Combat boots
16. Credit bureau
17. Catcher's box
18. Continental breakfast

174. MUTUAL REPLACEMENTS
1. Teller
2. Manned
3. Lilted
4. Collar
5. Gobble
6. Ferret
7. Romano
8. Paddle
9. Litter
10. Assert
11. Rodeos
12. Orders

175. DOUBLING BACK
1. Elbow, wobble
2. Salad, Dallas
3. Stews, sweets
4. Regan, nagger
5. Depot, topped
6. Sport, troops
7. Remus, summer
8. Degas, sagged
9. Sinus, Sunnis
10. Eager, reggae

176. TWO TREES
Balderdash

177. TAKING OFF THE CURVES
1. Fossil (foil)
2. Bossing (boing)
3. Possess (posse)
4. Lassos (Laos)
5. Classy (clay)
6. Needless (needle)
7. Mousse (moue)
8. Blessed (bleed)
9. Raciness (Racine)
10. Caresser (career)
11. Deadliness (deadline)
12. Blossom (bloom)

178. ADD-ONS
1. Bail, Bailey
2. Whisk, whiskey
3. Hick, hickey
4. Pull, pulley
5. Gall, galley
6. Troll, trolley
7. Hock, hockey
8. All, alley
9. Bog, bogey
10. Shell, Shelley

179. NEW TESTAMENT
1. Neaten
2. Tuition
3. Nation
4. Entente
5. Antenna
6. Nineteen
7. Intention
8. Antonio
9. Tenant
10. Antiunion
11. Annotation
12. Intuition
13. Intonation
14. Ten-to-one
15. Inattention
16. Antoinette

180. LONG GONE
Han Dynasty (handy + nasty)

181. HIGH SCHOOL LANGUAGE

1. Honor student
2. Hair salon
3. Hardware store
4. High society
5. "Hollywood Squares"
6. Ham sandwich
7. Hula skirt
8. Hoosier State
9. Horse show
10. Hot sauce
11. Hockey stick
12. Hunger strike
13. Head start
14. Home stretch
15. "Holy smokes!"

182. APPENDAGES

1. Host, hostage
2. Band, bandage
3. Aver, average
4. Mont, montage
5. Plum, plumage
6. Pill, pillage
7. Ramp, rampage
8. Mess, message
9. Foot, footage
10. Bond, bondage

183. PJ'S

1. Plain Jane
2. Pickle jar
3. Practical joke
4. Pope John
5. Poetic justice
6. Pearl Jam
7. Prune juice
8. Pea jacket
9. Paint job
10. "Pal Joey"
11. "Petticoat Junction"
12. Pizza joint

184. SOMETHING IN COMMON

A letter can be dropped from each word to leave a number (four, ten, thirty)

185. WHAT'S DOING?

1. Jumping
2. Shooting
3. Sleeping
4. Flying
5. Working
6. Sitting
7. Running
8. Driving
9. Moving
10. Fighting
11. Rolling
12. Passing
13. Playing
14. Laughing

186. PH SYSTEM

1. Panama hat
2. Pith helmet
3. Plow horse
4. Pinch hitter
5. Poker hand
6. Patrick Henry
7. Pearl Harbor
8. Purple Heart
9. Public housing
10. Plaza Hotel
11. Procol Harum
12. "Prizzi's Honor"
13. Publishing house
14. Pizza Hut
15. Publicity hound

187. TURNING HEADS

1. Same name came
2. Real veal meal
3. Sent gent rent
4. Pale Yale male
5. Fish dish wish
6. Mars bars jars
7. Hike like Mike
8. Long Hong Kong song
9. Call Pall Mall tall
10. Hill will kill bill

188. SADIST'S UNDOING

Easy does it

189. THICKET OF TREES

1. Maple
2. Birch
3. Pecan
4. Olive

5. Peach
6. Poplar
7. Locust
8. Orange
9. Willow
10. Laurel
11. Spruce
12. Apple, alder

190. MAKING GUESSES
1. Boxing gloves
2. Wedding gown
3. Chewing gum
4. Passing grade
5. Bowling Green
6. Letting go
7. Shooting gallery
8. Crossing guard
9. Starting gate
10. Laughing gas
11. "Crying Game"
12. "Amazing Grace"
13. Looking glass
14. Running gag
15. Landing gear
16. Smoking gun

191. AYE! AYE!
1. Dot, idiot
2. Lad, "Iliad"
3. Nut, Inuit
4. Tape, Taipei
5. Talc, italic
6. Dares, diaries
7. Chant, Chianti
8. Arness, airiness
9. Dante's, dainties
10. Fester, feistier

192. CITY AND STATE
Yonkers, New York

193. TWISTED MEANINGS
1. Begin
2. Cheap
3. Worth
4. Toper
5. Torso
6. Aches

7. Evict
8. Genre
9. Earth
10. Ideal
11. Nerve
12. Lucre
13. Marsh
14. Super

194. "CROSS" WORDS
1. Tax
2. Twenty-six
3. Thorax
4. Tom Mix
5. Triplex
6. Trail mix
7. Tux
8. T. Rex (Tyrannosaurus rex)
9. Trix
10. Tex-Mex
11. Tackle box
12. Timex
13. Turtle Wax
14. Tenor sax
15. Transfix
16. Thumb index

195. ONE AND THE SAME
1. Teach
2. Chapel
3. Referee
4. Select
5. Arrest
6. Err or error
7. Icy
8. Enrage
9. Veer
10. Shove
11. Shrub
12. Idiotic
13. Intellect
14. Aerials
15. Plenty
16. Ingesting
17. Tally
18. Astound or astonish

196. SOUND OF THE CITY
Nashville (Tenn.) and Asheville (N.C.)

197. EXTRA EFFORT

1. Easter egg
2. Electric eel
3. Emergency exit
4. Eastern Europe
5. Evil empire
6. Energy efficiency
7. Egyptian embassy
8. Entrance exam
9. En español
10. Elephant ears
11. Evening edition (or early edition)
12. Elementary education
13. English essayist
14. Electrical engineer
15. "Extra, extra!"

198. SMOOTH MOVE

1. Abroad
2. Caution
3. Trickle
4. Allergy
5. Iguana
6. Earthen
7. Accurse
8. Simmered
9. Wither
10. Unison
11. Begin, binge
12. Glare, lager

199. "IF I WERE U …"

1. Simmons, summons
2. Jingle, jungle
3. Sickle, suckle
4. Misty, musty
5. Diet, duet
6. Riffle, ruffle
7. Silly, sully
8. Stickup, stuck-up

200. PURE FICTION

Oedipus Rex

WHERE TO HEAR NPR'S *WEEKEND EDITION SUNDAY*

Nearly 500 public radio stations throughout the United States carry *Weekend Edition Sunday* as this book goes to press. Below is a list of the stations, organized by state. The two-hour program is heard on Sunday morning in most locales. (For the exact time on the station nearest you, go to <www.npr.org/programs/wesun>; click "Where to hear.") On most stations the puzzle begins at 40 minutes into the first hour. Note: All stations below are FM except those marked by an asterisk (*).

Alabama
Birmingham—WBHM (90.3)
Dothan—WRWA (88.7)
Gadsden—WSGN (91.5)
Huntsville—WLRH (89.3)
Jacksonville—WLJS (91.9)
Muscle Shoals—WQPR (88.7)
Selma—WAPR (88.3)
Troy—WTSU (89.9)
Tuscaloosa—WUAL (91.5)

Alaska
Anchorage—KSKA (91.1)
Anchorage—KSRD (88.1)
Barrow—KBRW (91.9)
Bethel—KYUK (*640)
Chevak—KCUK (88.1)
Fairbanks—KUAC (104.7)
Galena—KIYU (*910)
Glennallen—KXGA (90.5)
Haines—KHNS (102.3)
Homer—KBBI (*890)
Juneau—KTOO (104.3)
Kenai—KDLL (91.9)
Ketchikan—KRBD (105.9)
Kodiak—KMXT (100.1)
McCarthy—KXKM (89.7)
Petersburg—KFSK (100.9)
Sitka—KCAW (104.7)
St. Paul—KUHB (91.9)
Talkeetna—KTNA (88.5)
Valdez—KCHU (*770)

Arizona
Flagstaff—KNAQ (91.7)
Flagstaff—KNAU (88.7)
Page—KNAD (91.7)
Phoenix—KJZZ (91.5)
Prescott—KPUB (89.3)
Show Low—KNAA (90.7)
Tucson—KUAT (*1550)
Tucson—KUAZ (89.1)

Yuma—KAWC (*1320)
Yuma—KAWC (88.9)

Arkansas
El Dorado—KBSA (90.9)
Fayetteville—KUAF (91.3)
Jonesboro—KASU (91.9)
Little Rock—KUAR (89.1)

California
Arcata—KHSU (90.5)
Bakersville—KPRX (89.1)
Burney—KNCA (89.7)
Chico—KCHO (91.7)
Crescent City—KHSR (91.1)
Fresno—KVPR (89.3)
Indio—KCRY (89.3)
Mt. Shasta—KNSQ (88.1)
Oxnard—KCRU (89.1)
Pacific Grove—KAZU (90.3)
Pasadena—KPCC (89.3)
Philo—KZYX (90.7)
Redding—KFPR (88.9)
Rohnert Park—KRCB (91.1)
Sacramento—KXJZ (88.9)
San Bernardino—KVCR (91.9)
San Diego—KPBS (89.5)
San Francisco—KQED (88.5)
San Luis Obispo—KCBX (90.1)
Santa Cruz—KUSP (88.9)
Santa Monica—KCRW (89.9)
Stockton—KUOP (91.3)
Tahoe City—KKTO (90.5)
Thousand Oaks—KCLU (88.3)
Willits—KZYZ (91.5)
Yreka—KNYR (91.3)

Colorado
Alamosa—KRZA (88.7)
Aspen—KAJX (91.5)
Colorado Springs—KRCC (91.5)

Cortez—KSJD (91.5)
Crested Butte—KBUT (90.3)
Denver—KCFR (90.1)
Grand Junction—KPRN (89.5)
Greeley—KUNC (91.5)
Ignacio—KSUT (91.3)
Montrose—KPRH (88.3)
Paonia—KVNF (90.9)
Pueblo—KCFP (91.9)
Telluride—KOTO (91.7)
Vail—KPRE (89.9)

Connecticut
Westport—WMMM (*1260)

District of Columbia
Washington—WETA (90.9)

Florida
Fort Myers—WGCU (90.1)
Fort Pierce—WQCS (88.9)
Gainesville—WUFT (89.1)
Inverness—WJUF (90.1)
Melbourne—WFIT (89.5)
Miami—WLRN (91.3)
Panama City—WFSW (89.1)
Panama City—WKGC (90.7)
Pensacola—WUWF (88.1)
Tallahassee—WFSU (88.9)
Tampa—WUSF (89.7)
West Palm Beach—WXEL (90.7)

Georgia
Albany—WUNV (91.7)
Athens—WUGA (91.7)
Atlanta—WJSP (88.1)
Augusta—WACG (90.7)
Brunswick—WWIO (89.1)
Carrollton—WWGC (90.7)
Columbus—WTJB (91.7)
Dahlonega—WNGU (89.5)
Demorest—WPPR (88.3)

Fort Gaines—WJWV (90.9)
Macon—WDCO (89.7)
Savannah—WSVH (91.1)
Tifton—WABR (91.1)
Valdosta—WWET (91.7)
Waycross—WXVS (90.1)

Guam
Mangiloa—KPRG (89.3)

Hawaii
Honolulu—KIPO (89.3)
Pearl City—KIFO (*1380)

Idaho
Boise—KBSX (91.5)
Cottonwood—KNWO (90.1)
Rexburg—KRIC (100.5)
Twin Falls—KBSW (91.7)

Illinois
Carbondale—WSIU (91.9)
Chicago—WBEZ (91.5)
DeKalb—WNIJ (90.5)
Macomb—WIUM (91.3)
Normal—WGLT (89.1)
Olney—WUSI (90.3)
Peoria—WCBU (89.9)
Pittsfield—WIPA (89.3)
Quincy—WQUB (90.3)
Rock Island—WVIK (90.3)
Springfield—WUIS (91.9)
Urbana—WILL (*580)
Warsaw—WIUW (89.5)

Indiana
Anderson—WBSB (89.5)
Bloomington—WFIU (103.7)
Crawfordsville—WVXI (106.3)
Elkhart—WVPE (88.1)
Evansville—WNIN (88.3)
Hagerstown—WBSH (91.1)
Indianapolis—WFYI (90.1)
Marian—WBSW (90.9)
Muncie—WBST (92.1)
Portland—WBSJ (91.7)
Richmond—WVXR (89.3)
West Lafayette—WBAA (*920)

Iowa
Ames—WOI (*640)
Cedar Falls—KUNI (90.9)

Decorah—KLNI (88.7)
Fort Dodge—KTPR (91.1)
Iowa City—WSUI (*910)
Mason City—KUNY (91.5)
Sioux City—KWIT (90.3)

Kansas
Garden City—KANZ (91.1)
Great Bend—KHCT (90.9)
Hill City—KZNA (90.5)
Hutchinson—KHCC (90.1)
Lawrence—KANU (91.5)
Pittsburg—KRPS (89.9)
Salina—KHCD (89.5)
Wichita—KMUW (89.1)

Kentucky
Bowling Green—WKYU (88.9)
Elizabethtown—WKUE (90.9)
Hazard—WEKH (90.9)
Henderson—WKPB (89.5)
Lexington—WUKY (91.3)
Louisville—WFPL (89.3)
Morehead—WMKY (90.3)
Murray—WKMS (91.3)
Richmond—WEKU (88.9)
Somerset—WDCL (89.7)

Louisiana
Alexandria—KLSA (90.7)
Baton Rouge—WRKF (89.3)
Monroe—KEDM (90.3)
New Orleans—WWNO (89.9)
Shreveport—KDAQ (89.9)
Thibodaux—KTLN (90.5)

Maine
Bangor—WMEH (90.9)
Calais—WMED (89.7)
Fort Kent—WMEF (106.5)
Portland/Lewiston—WMEA
  (90.1)
Presque Isle—WMEM (106.1)
Waterville—WMEW (91.3)

Mariana Islands
Saipan—KRNM (88.1)

Maryland
Baltimore—WJHU (88.1)
Ocean City—WSDL (90.7)
Salisbury—WSCL (89.5)

Massachusetts
Boston—WBUR (90.9)
Great Barrington—WAMQ
  (105.1)
Harwich—WCCT (90.3)
Sandwich—WSDH (91.5)
West Barnstable—WKKL
  (90.7)
West Yarmouth—WBUR
  (*1240)

Michigan
Alpena—WCML (91.7)
Ann Arbor—WUOM (91.7)
Bay City—WUCX (90.1)
Detroit—WDET (101.9)
East Lansing—WKAR (*870)
Flint—WFUM (91.1)
Grand Rapids—WGVU
  (*1480)
Grand Rapids—WGVU
  (88.5)
Grand Rapids—WVGR
  (104.1)
Harbor Springs—WCMW
  (103.9)
Houghton—WGGL (91.9)
Kalamazoo—WMUK (102.1)
Manistee—WVXM (97.7)
Marquette—WNMU (90.1)
Mt. Pleasant—WCMU (89.5)
Oscoda—WCMB (95.7)
Rogers City—WVXA (96.7)
Sault Ste. Marie—WCMZ
  (98.3)
Ypsilanti—WEMU (89.1)

Minnesota
Appleton—KNCM (88.5)
Bemidji—KNBJ (91.3)
Buhl—WIRN (92.5)
Collegeville—KNSR (88.9)
Duluth—WSCN (100.5)
Grand Rapids—KAXE (91.7)
La Crescent—KXLC (91.1)
Moorhead—KCCD (90.3)
Rochester—KZSE (90.7)
St. Paul—KNOW (91.1)
St. Peter—KNGA (91.5)
Thief River Falls—KNTN
  (102.7)
Worthington—KNSW (91.7)

Mississippi
Biloxi—WMAH (90.3)
Booneville—WMAE (89.5)
Bude—WMAU (88.9)
Greenwood—WMAO (90.9)
Jackson—WMPN (91.3)
Meridian—WMAW (88.1)
Mississippi State—WMAB
   (89.9)
Oxford—WMAV (90.3)
Senatobia—WKNA (88.9)

Missouri
Branson—KSMS (90.5)
Cape Girardeau—KRCU
   (90.9)
Chillicothe—KRNW (88.9)
Columbia—KBIA (91.3)
Kansas City—KCUR (89.3)
Maryville—KXCV (90.5)
Rolla—KUMR (88.5)
Springfield—KSMU (91.1)
St. Louis—KWMU (90.7)
Warrensburg—KCMW
   (90.9)

Montana
Billings—KEMC (91.7)
Bozeman—KBMC (102.1)
Great Falls—KGPR (89.9)
Harlem—KGVA (88.1)
Havre—KNMC (90.1)
Miles City—KECC (90.7)
Missoula—KUFM (89.1)

Nebraska
Alliance—KTNE (91.1)
Bassett—KMNE (90.3)
Chadron—KCNE (91.9)
Hastings—KHNE (89.1)
Lexington—KLNE (88.7)
Lincoln—KUCV (90.9)
Merriman—KRNE (91.5)
Norfolk—KXNE (89.3)
North Platte—KPNE (91.7)
Omaha—KIOS (91.5)

Nevada
Elko—KNCC (91.5)
Las Vegas—KNPR (89.5)
Panaca—KLNR (91.7)
Reno—KUNR (88.7)
Tonopah—KTPH (91.7)

New Hampshire
Concord—WEVO (89.1)
Hanover—WEVH (91.3)
Keene—WEVN (90.7)

New Jersey
Atlantic City—WNJN (89.7)
Berlin—WNJS (88.1)
Bridgeton—WNJB (89.3)
Lincroft—WBJB (90.5)
Sussex—WNJP (88.5)
Trenton—WNJT (88.1)

New Mexico
Albuquerque—KUNM (89.9)
Gallup—KGLP (91.7)
Las Cruces—KRWG (90.7)
Maljamar—KMTH (98.7)
Portales—KENW (89.5)
Ramah-Pine Hill—KTDB (89.7)

New York
Albany—WAMC (90.3)
Binghamton—WSKG (89.3)
Binghamton—WSQX (91.5)
Blue Mountain Lake—WXLH
   (91.3)
Buffalo—WBFO (88.7)
Buffalo—WNED (*970)
Canajoharie—WCAN (93.3)
Canton—WSLU (89.5)
Corning—WSQE (91.1)
Geneva—WEOS (89.7)
Ithaca—WSQG (90.9)
Jamestown—WUBJ (88.1)
Jeffersonville—WJFF (90.5)
Kingston—WAMK (90.9)
Malone—WSLO (90.9)
Middletown—WOSR (91.7)
New York—WNYC (*820)
New York—WNYC (93.9)
North Creek—WXLG (89.9)
Olean—WOLN (91.3)
Oneonta—WSQC (91.7)
Oswego—WRVO (89.9)
Peru—WXLU (88.3)
Plattsburgh—WCEL (91.9)
Rochester—WXXI (*1370)
Saranac Lake—WSLL (90.5)
Selden—WSUF (89.9)
Ticonderoga—WANC (103.9)
Utica—WRVN (91.9)
Watertown—WRVJ (91.7)

Watertown—WSLJ (88.9)

North Carolina
Asheville—WCQS (88.1)
Chapel Hill—WUNC (91.5)
Charlotte—WFAE (90.7)
Fayetteville—WFSS (91.9)
Franklin—WFQS (91.3)
Hickory—WFHE (90.3)
Kinston—WKNS (90.5)
New Bern—WTEB (89.3)
Rocky Mountain—WRQM
   (90.9)
Spindale—WNCW (88.7)
Wilmington—WHQR (91.3)
Winston-Salem—WFDD
   (88.5)

North Dakota
Bismarck—KCND (90.5)
Dickinson—KDPR (89.9)
Fargo—KDSU (91.9)
Grand Forks—KUND (89.3)
Jamestown—KPRJ (91.5)
Minot—KMPR (88.9)
Williston—KPPR (89.5)

Ohio
Athens—WOUB (*1340)
Athens—WOUB (91.3)
Bryan—WGBE (90.9)
Cambridge—WOUC (89.1)
Chillicothe—WOUH (91.9)
Chillicothe—WVXC (89.3)
Cincinnati—WVXU (91.7)
Cleveland—WCPN (90.3)
Columbus—WCBE (90.5)
Columbus—WOSU (*820)
Ironton—WOUL (89.1)
Kent—WKSU (89.7)
Lima—WGLE (90.7)
Mt. Gilead—WVXG (95.1)
New Philadelphia—WKRJ
   (91.5)
Oxford—WMUB (88.5)
Thompson—WKSV (89.1)
Toledo—WGTE (91.3)
West Union—WVXW (89.5)
Wooster—WKRW (89.3)
Yellow Springs—WYSO
   (91.3)
Youngstown—WYSU (88.5)
Zanesville—WOUZ (90.1)

Oklahoma
Ardmore—KLCU (90.3)
Lawton—KCCU (89.3)
Norman—KGOU (106.3)
Oklahoma City—KROU (105.7)
Stillwater—KOSU (91.7)
Tulsa—KWGS (89.5)

Oregon
Ashland—KSMF (89.1)
Ashland—KSOR (90.1)
Ashland—KSRG (88.3)
Bend—KOAB (91.3)
Coos Bay—KSBA (88.5)
Eugene—KLCC (89.7)
Klamath Falls—KSKF (90.9)
Newport—KLCO (90.5)
Pendleton—KRBM (90.9)
Portland—KOAC (*550)
Portland—KOPB (91.5)
Roseburg—KSRS (91.5)

Pennsylvania
Bethlehem—WDIY (88.1)
Erie—WQLN (91.3)
Harrisburg—WITF (89.5)
Kane—WPSB (90.1)
Philadelphia—WHYY (90.9)
Pittsburgh—WDUQ (90.5)
Pittston—WVIA (89.9)
University Park—WPSU (91.5)

Rhode Island
North Providence—WRNI (*1290)
Westerley—WXNI (*1230)

South Carolina
Aiken—WLJK (89.1)
Beaufort—WJWJ- (89.9)
Charleston—WSCI (89.3)
Columbia—WLTR- (91.3)
Conway—WHMC (90.1)
Greenville—WEPR (90.1)
Rock Hill—WNSC (88.9)
Sumter—WRJA (88.1)

South Dakota
Brookings—KESD (88.3)
Faith—KPSD (97.1)
Lowry—KQSD (91.9)
Martin—KZSD (102.5)
Pierpont—KDSD (90.9)
Rapid City—KBHE (89.3)
Reliance—KTSD (91.1)
Sioux Falls—KCSD (90.9)
Vermillion—KUSD (89.7)

Tennessee
Chattanooga—WUTC (88.1)
Cookeville—WHRS (91.7)
Dyersburg—WKNQ (90.7)
Jackson—WKNP (90.1)
Johnson City—WETS (89.5)
Memphis—WKNO (91.1)
Nashville—WPLN (*1430)
Nashville—WPLN (90.3)

Texas
Abilene—KACU (89.7)
Austin—KUT (90.5)
Beaumont—KVLU (91.3)
College Station—KAMU (90.9)
Corpus Christi—KEDT (90.3)
Dallas—KERA (90.1)
El Paso—KTEP (88.5)
Harlingen—KMBH (88.9)
Houston—KUHF (88.7)
Ingram—KTXI (90.1)
Lubbock—KOHM (89.1)
McAllen—KHID (88.1)
Odessa—KOCV (91.3)
Redland—KLDN (88.9)
San Angelo—KUTX (90.1)
San Antonio—KSTX (89.1)
Texarkana—KTXK (91.5)
Victoria—KVRT (90.7)
Waco—KWBU (103.3)

Utah
Coalville—KCUA (92.5)
Logan—KUSU (91.5)
Park City—KPCW (91.9)
Salt Lake City—KCPW (88.3)
Salt Lake City—KUER (90.1)

Vermont
Colchester—WVPS (107.9)
Rutland—WRVT (88.7)
Windsor—WVPR (89.5)

Virginia
Blacksburg—WVTW (88.5)
Charlottesville—WVTU (89.3)
Crozet—WMRY (103.5)
Harrisonburg—WMRA (90.7)
Lexington—WMRL (89.9)
Marian—WVTR (91.9)
Norfolk—WHRV (89.5)
Richmond—WCVE (88.9)
Roanoke—WVTF (89.1)

Washington
Bellingham—KZAZ (91.7)
Clarkston—KNWV (90.5)
Ellensburg—KNWR (90.7)
Moses Lake—KLWS (91.5)
Port Angeles—KNWP (90.1)
Pullman—KRFA (91.7)
Pullman—KWSU (*1250)
Richland—KFAE (89.1)
Seattle—KUOW (94.9)
Spokane—KPBX (91.1)
Spokane—KSFC (91.9)
Tacoma—KPLU (88.5)
Walla Walla—KWWS (89.7)
Yakima—KNWY (90.3)

West Virginia
Beckley—WVPB (91.7)
Buckhannon—WVPW (88.9)
Charleston—WVPN (88.5)
Huntington—WVWV (89.9)
Martinsburg—WVEP (88.9)
Morgantown—WVPM (90.9)
Parkersburg—WVPG (90.3)
Petersburg—WAUA (89.5)
Wheeling—WVNP (89.9)

Wisconsin
Brule—WHSA (89.9)
Eau Claire—WUEC (89.7)
Green Bay—WPNE (89.3)
Hayward—WOJB (88.9)
Kenosha—WGTD (91.1)
LaCrosse—WLSU (88.9)
Madison—WERN (88.7)
Menomonie—WVSS (90.7)
Milwaukee—WUWM (89.7)
Wausau—WHRM (90.9)

Wyoming
Afton—KUWA (91.3)
Casper—KUWC (91.3)
Gillette—KUWG (90.9)
Jackson—KUWJ (90.3)
Laramie—KUWR (91.9)
Newcastle—KUWN (90.5)
Rock Springs—KUWZ (90.5)
Sheridan—KSUW (91.3)